· A TASTE FOR ·

ABSINTHE

· A TASTE FOR ·

ABSINTHE

65 *Recipes for Classic & Contemporary Cocktails*

R. WINSTON GUTHRIE

with JAMES F. THOMPSON

Photography by LIZA GERSHMAN

Clarkson Potter/Publishers
New York

Published in the United States by Clarkson Potter/Publishers,
an imprint of the Crown Publishing Group, a division of
Random House, Inc., New York.
www.crownpublishing.com
www.clarksonpotter.com

CLARKSON POTTER is a trademark and POTTER with
colophon is a registered trademark of Random House, Inc.

Library of Congress Cataloging-in-Publication Data
Guthrie, R. Winston.
A taste for absinthe / R. Winston Guthrie, with James F.
Thompson, and Liza Gershman.——1st ed.
Includes index.
1. Cocktails.   2. Absinthe.   I. Thompson, James F.   II.
Gershman, Liza.   III. Title.
TX951.G845 2010
641.8′74——dc22   2009045578

ISBN 978-0-307-58753-4

Printed in China

Design by Laura Palese

10   9   8   7   6   5   4   3   2   1

First Edition

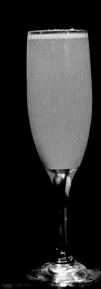

RIGHT: *Death + Company's Brian Miller created
the North by Northwest* [recipe on page 105].

FRONTISPIECE: *Erika Fey created the Heart Grows
Fonder* [recipe on page 128].

DEDICATION

TO MEREDITH, MY WIFE & BEST FRIEND
——who keeps me looking up at the stars

· ·

· ACKNOWLEDGMENTS ·

I WOULD LIKE TO GIVE SPECIAL THANKS TO ALL THE WONDERFUL & TALENTED PEOPLE WHO CONTRIBUTED TO OR INFLUENCED THIS BOOK:

Absinthe experts and friends John Troia and Peter Schaf [owners of Tempus Fugit Spirits and Vieux Pontarlier Absinthe] were insightful, generous with resources and contacts, and always ready to help. On the forefront of the absinthe renaissance in America, they were also generous with their time and knowledge. Thanks to Jeff Hollinger for broadening the scope of the book. Special thanks to Scott Baird and Tim Stookey. Thanks to all of the other bartenders who made recipes specifically for this project. Thanks to Liza Gershman, who was instrumental in conceptualizing much of the book as she went above and beyond the role of photographer. Thanks to Andrea Somberg, Jim Thompson, Ashley Phillips, Rosy Ngo, Laura Palese, and Amy Sly for their dedication to the project and belief that Absinthe has something to offer everyone in America. Special thanks to the absinthe community and all those in search of the Green Fairy.

Enjoy your journey . . .

ABSINTHE DÉCHANET

Gustave Déchanet Fils

PONTARLIER (DOUBS)

CONTENTS

FOREWORD

Absinthe's rise and fall is a colorful story that has been chronicled before, but the romance and mystery of the "Green Fairy" hasn't been fully captured until now. *A Taste for Absinthe* explores its history in the Old World and in American cocktails and breaks new ground with dozens of inventive cocktail recipes.

Throughout the nineteenth century, absinthe became the most popular and widely consumed spirit in Europe. Yet by the end of the same century, several countries had banned the drink, labeling it as highly addictive and poisonous. The unfolding story of its rebirth resulting from the easing of official bans around the globe comes alive in sidebars that accompany the recipes. But the real strength of *A Taste for Absinthe* lies in the collection of amazing recipes elicited from talented bartenders who are part of an emerging group referred to as *cocktailian* bartenders. Cocktailians are professionals and sometimes gifted amateurs dedicated to exploring the history of cocktail tradition, mastering techniques, and developing product knowledge to an extent heretofore unprecedented in the bartending community.

The authors have provided for the first time in print a collection of modern absinthe recipes with notes from the cocktailian inventors discussing their ingredient choices and their inspiration. The pages of this book provide a unique look into the minds of the most innovative bartenders working today. There are also many fine photographs that show retro ephemera——from glasses and spoons to fountains——as well as cocktail presentations employed in many cutting-edge bars located across the country.

A Taste for Absinthe is an indispensable handbook to creating world-class cocktails using this once-illicit drink. Cheers to a job well done.

——Dale DeGroff, aka King Cocktail,
author of *The Craft of the Cocktail* and *The Essential Cocktail*

*Ryan Fitzgerald at Baretta makes the
Third Degree [recipe on page 99]*

INTRODUCTION

Absinthe is one of the most mysterious elixirs of modern history. Considering the centuries of negative innuendo and misrepresentation that have plagued absinthe, it is not surprising that the beverage suffers from widespread suspicion and poor public relations. Times, however, are about to change——absinthe is finally having its day in the American court of public opinion. With the reversal of a century-long ban on absinthe and the recent production of American-made absinthe now on shelves, the Green Fairy no longer needs to rely on her historical ambassadors——Vincent van Gogh, Pablo Picasso, Henri de Toulouse-Lautrec, Oscar Wilde, and Ernest Hemingway, to name a few.

Tastemakers in some of the country's hottest culinary epicenters have been beguiled by absinthe's sophisticated flavor profile and are incorporating it into cocktails that pay homage to the elixir's rich and storied history while appealing to contemporary palates. From Los Angeles and Napa Valley to Boston and New York, the appeal of absinthe is being rediscovered in bars and restaurants. Perhaps it may be just a matter of time until Americans celebrate absinthe the way the Green Goddess was celebrated in the cafés and bars of Paris, resulting in a Belle Époque phenomenon known as l'Heure Verte, or the Green Hour, where absinthe enthusiasts——mostly artists and intellectuals——met to socialize and discuss matters of the heart, soul, and mind.

Today real——yes, *real*——absinthe is back, and poised to make a splash in the United States. Absinthe's second coming has quickly grown into a culinary movement; bars, restaurants, liquor stores, and drinkers across America are setting out their slotted spoons and sugar cubes, and filling their absinthe fountains with ice as the drink is stirring up the cocktail industry. After being accused of sinking entire populations into crazed, bug-eyed convulsions, the widespread vilification of absinthe is coming to an end. Now, the Green Fairy is finally being properly sipped as the engines of pop culture——movies,

music, books, and the Internet——bring it back into the mainstream.

With the help of master mixologists at your fingertips, *A Taste for Absinthe* offers you sixty-five recipes to discover the charms of the Green Fairy. Readers can approach the content in a needs-based manner, looking up particular recipes based on the ingredients featured in specific chapters, or read the book straight through for a complete perspective on the compelling history and exciting modern recipes that utilize absinthe. Each recipe includes a brief description of what makes it unique followed by a list of ingredients and an easy-to-follow, step-by-step explanation of how to prepare each drink. World-renowned absinthe experts, such as Jeff Hollinger and Jim Meehan, offer insider insights and mixology tips on how to best prepare and enjoy absinthe. From traditional practices to cutting-edge recipes, the following pages offer everything the absinthe drinker needs to know in order to serve and enjoy absinthe for any occasion, any time of the year.

The Bitter End, created by Josh Harris from the Bon Vivantes [recipe on pages 54—55].

ABSINTHE PRIMER

Long veiled in mystery and intrigue——with rumors making up what most people these days think this drink is——absinthe is slowly shedding its false identity. Many of the ingredients in authentic absinthe are unfamiliar merely because we don't often encounter them. A primer explaining the mysterious herbal mixture that's key to the drink's flavor will help dispel the fear that absinthe is a bewitching elixir.

In the nineteenth century, absinthe was originally taken neat as a medicine, in very small doses [like most alcoholic/herbal tinctures, which were normally diluted into water or dripped onto a cube of sugar or possibly mixed with honey]. Around 1830, before any popularly known uses of absinthe as an aperitif, the French army provided absinthe to its soldiers fighting in Algeria. Drinking water was notoriously unclean in desert or tropical zones [and even, at that time, in Paris!], so wine, beer, or diluted spirits were often consumed in lieu of pure water. Prescribed drops of absinthe per cup of water eventually increased, and the ratio was actually reversed when it was found that the herbal alcohol helped ease the pains of war. The soldiers soon discovered that absinthe tasted better when the water was more deliberately and methodically added to the alcohol; thus they developed the classic absinthe drip [see page 29].

ABSINTHE'S LIBERATION

The bans on absinthe began in the early 1900s. In the United States, bad press from across the Atlantic and an anti-absinthe novel——*Wormwood: A Drama of Paris* by Marie Corelli [who was the Belle Époque equivalent of a Danielle Steele-type novelist]—— caused a furor among the public. Absinthe was mostly consumed in cities such as San Francisco, New Orleans, Chicago, and New York, but scandalous stories spread across America, prompting the government's ban in 1912 for "protective" measures.

It took until the late 1980s for absinthe to begin to be accepted again. In 1988, the French government passed a decree based on World Health Organization protocols that, in effect, relegalized absinthe by defining the limit of the chemicals that were thought to be dangerous——those naturally found in wormwood, fennel, and hyssop. Today it is required for absinthe to undergo a chemical analysis for thujone, fenchone, and pino camphone limits, and in France it also must follow certain labeling guidelines.

The "relegalization" of absinthe in the United States followed many petitions sent to the U.S. government by Swiss and American interests over a period of about five years, asking for an explanation of the legality of its prohibition. The efforts prevailed, and as of 2007, absinthe has been accepted for distribution and manufacture in the United States. Absinthe production follows similar definitions and limitations as in the European Union on the quantity of thujone.

In 1943, absinthe appeared in the film based on the Ernest Hemingway novel *For Whom the Bell Tolls*. Robert Jordan, the lead character played by Gary Cooper, is assigned a dangerous mission: to blow up a bridge in the mountains of Spain during the Civil War. He reaches for absinthe in his most desperate hour.

ABSINTHE'S UNIQUE FLAVOR

Absinthe was classically defined by the use of the Holy Trinity of herbs as its flavor base: Grande absinthe [wormwood], green anise seed [star anise is sometimes substituted but not as fine], and fennel seed. Other herbs and spices can be added to suit individual distillers' palates or reflect regional tastes. These ingredients were added to a neutral [clean and almost flavorless] base spirit——grape alcohol was considered the highest quality, though grain and beet alcohols have been used. A well-made absinthe will have a complex bouquet of herbal and floral aromas as a result of the combination of both distilled and coloring herbs——sometimes reminiscent of a fresh, springtime Alpine meadow with crisp bright flavors, and other times being more warm and spicy, depending on the recipe.

The first aromatic impression that an American taster picks up is that of licorice. Most high-quality absinthes do not contain licorice; the flavors of anise and fennel seed are similar to that of licorice. The anise profile should not be overbearing——though it can be when star anise or too much green anise is used——but should provide a sweet and fresh background. The aroma of wormwood at its finest is lightly mentholated and can have an earthy-heady aspect. Ironically, the aroma is rarely encountered in modern absinthes and is often confused by inexperienced tasters as a defect.

There is some necessary bitterness in good absinthe, but it is a balanced herbal undertone, and not overpowering. Traditional absinthe is an anise-based spirit. Nonanise, or "low-licorice-tasting," absinthes were recently made under the presumption that the American palate is unacquainted with or dislikes anise-flavored alcohols and that more people would drink absinthe without this flavor. It is much like making Islay Scotch without any peat: people want to say they drink Islay Scotch, but they don't like the taste and smell of peat, though it's the drink's characteristic flavor.

WORMWOOD

Wormwood [*Artemisia absinthium*] is a plant related to sagebrush. It's also known in French as Grande absinthe, as it is the principal defining ingredient of the beverage and where the name is derived. It grows wild in many regions of the world, but is found in abundance in sunny, cool, mountainous areas, specifically the Jura Mountains of Eastern France on the border shared with Switzerland.

There are several varietals of Grande absinthe, some extremely aromatic and flavorful, and others very muted and dull. Wormwood is naturally very bitter, but most of this bitterness is removed during distillation. However, a well-made absinthe will always have a slight but pleasurable bitterness, appreciated just as in a fine Italian espresso or a dark chocolate. The best plants are harvested just before the flowers at their tops have opened, thus optimally preserving the aromatic qualities. Wormwood has been used historically in many alcoholic preparations throughout Europe. For example, the German word for wormwood is *vermut*, which shows the connection to the use of wormwood as a bittering agent in vermouth.

THE MYTH OF HALLUCINATIONS

Absinthe has many times been condemned as a danger-ous drug——one that plunges drinkers into hallucina-tory spells. Yet we now know that the threat of such effects is unfounded——or, rather, only mildly cor-rect. The chemical thujone can be blamed, but this naturally occurring substance is potentially harmful only in extremely high doses. Therefore, there are strict regulations in place to ensure that absinthe is now made with safe levels of thujone.

A fragrant and oily chemical, thujone is found in various plants, notably wormwood, as well as in sage, tansy, tarragon, and the bark of the thuja tree, from where it gets its name. In high does, it is believed to be a neurotoxin. The liquor absinthe is not thujone——in fact, very little thujone actually finds its way into distilled absinthe. Early research-ers generally tested wormwood oil, a highly concen-trated extract, for levels of thujone. Some recent researchers assumed that thujone was present in high quantities in nineteenth-century absinthes, but others found that this wasn't the case. Previously unopened antique bottles of absinthe as well as modern absinthes distilled according to historical protocols have been tested and they show extremely low levels of thujone, most often well within the amount allowed by EU regulations.

In extremely high doses, thujone is dangerous, but the concentration of thujone actu-ally found in the beverage absinthe is nothing to worry about. You would need to drink seven liters [!] of the undiluted spirit to have any adverse effect directly from thujone. The alcohol, and even the water [if you diluted it], would kill you before!

· TOUCH OF THE ·
GREEN
FAIRY

An urban legend regarding absinthe is that it has drug-like effects. The reality is that absinthe is a high-alcohol spirit that has attributes of a depressant [alcohol] and a stimulant [ane-thole from anise]. The combina-tion can cause, in some drinkers, a "secondary effect," different from drunkenness, which is a "wide-awake" feeling, attributed to the anethole. One could also say that tequila produces a differ-ent drunken feeling [secondary effect] than beer, whisky, or wine.

Thujone was discovered and isolated to absinthe during the nineteenth century to make it "different" from other spirits, in order to condemn and ban it. This movement was headed by the antialcohol leagues and winegrowers unions, who saw all high-proof spirits, but especially absinthe, as a threat. Unfortunately, modern absinthes are now being marketed with thujone as a selling point, proffering the idea of the supposed "drug-like" effects while smoke-screening poorly made products and hindering the development of absinthe as a high-quality spirit.

ABSINTHE'S ALLURING GREEN TINT

The color of absinthe is a secondary effect of the maceration of various herbs into the colorless extract after distillation. Historically, absinthe was green, amber, or clear and exhibited an underlying sweetness produced by macerating fresh herbs in a warm bath of neutral spirit and distilling. This primary distillation produced an aromatic *blanche,* or clear, absinthe rich in flavors. *Verte,* or green, absinthe would go through a second process that infused additional herbs to enhance its flavor profile——as a result, chlorophyll from the herbs was left behind, giving absinthe its green tint. The final color is determined by the types and amounts of herbs infused and mellows with age and turns an amber-green, called *feuille morte,* or "dead leaf." Artificial colorings or dyes were fairly common in cheaper absinthes but not used by the best producers.

THE LOUCHE

The *louche* is the cloud that forms when water is dripped into absinthe. The slow addition of cold water to absinthe causes a reaction that allows essential oils to precipitate out of their suspension in the high alcohol content, releasing the aromas and flavors that are so appreciated by the absintheur. The anethole from anise and fennel seed can start to crystallize at a temperature less than 20 degrees centigrade, causing an additional whiteness in the cooling liquid from the slow formation of crystals. Depending on the type and concentration of essences and alcohol percentage, the clouding effect can be quick forming and milky thick white, to lightly opaque with opalescent reflections. The most desirable louches are slow-forming yet deliberate milky trails caused by the water dropping through the absinthe, gradually forming a moderately opaque drink with reflections of the original green color of the undiluted absinthe. Though many consider thick louches to be a sign of the absinthe's strength and quality, it can also signify the

overuse of anethole-rich star anise, which can numb tastebuds and result in a distractingly one-dimensional flavor. Too much anethole stuns the palate and makes the absinthe much harder to appreciate than more subtle aromatic qualities.

"FAKE" VS. "REAL" ABSINTHE

For the sake of an understandable definition, "real" absinthe is defined as a typical high-quality absinthe product, similar to that which was produced during the Belle Époque by such brands such as Pernod Fils. Real absinthe should be a liquor of no less than 50 percent alcohol [100 proof] that is not presweetened and contains wormwood [*Artemisia absinthium*], anise [preferably green anise seed and/or to a lesser degree, badiane, or star anise], and fennel seed. It should turn cloudy [louche, or "trouble"] with the addition of cold water.

Again, for the sake of an understandable definition, "fake" absinthe is defined as a product that is not produced in accordance with historical distilling methods or ingredients. Fake absinthe is most commonly high-proof base alcohol with artificial green color [often bright or even neon green color]. It typically does not louche with the addition of water and is often extremely bitter with or without water. An herbal drink, even with wormwood, that does not contain a noticeable anise profile and does not noticeably cloud when ice water is added should not be considered a traditional or even a real absinthe. Most Bohemian-style absinthes have little or no anise in them [as this is not an appreci-

The origin of a particular brand of absinthe shouldn't be a major concern, as long as it is produced using high-quality herbs, alcohol, and distilling apparatuses. However, from a historic perspective, the best absinthes were made in the Jura region of eastern France, in particular the city of Pontarlier and the Val-de-Travers region of Switzerland, which almost borders Pontarlier.

ated taste in Eastern Europe] and as such, do not cloud, but typically become insipidly diluted when water is added. This bears no resemblance to traditional absinthe and would have been considered a major defect during the époque.

There are, however, different colored and uncolored types of absinthes that are produced in a variety of methods, including those that are distilled, compounded [oil-mix], and macerated.

MODERN ABSINTHE

The vast majority of modern absinthes bears little resemblance to original absinthe of the nineteenth century. However, a handful are virtually identical.

Historic recipes have been found in handwritten protocols held by still-functioning distilleries and in antique distiller's manuals, some even dating into the eighteenth century. Some of these recipes have been followed exactly——using wormwood from the same historic region, the same additional ingredients, and the same alembic stills and techniques of distillation and coloration——resulting in absinthes that are remarkably authentic. However, there are many modern producers who claim to use the traditional ingredients and processes for making absinthe but actually only add flavorings and dyes to alcohol. To know you're getting the real deal, it's important to research what you're buying.

One aspect of absinthe that was vitally important during the Absinthe Époque was the *terroir* [origin] of the wormwood plants used in distillation. Extremely fragrant wormwood from the mountain plateau of Pontarlier in Eastern France was so highly prized that demand often outstripped the harvests. Presently, there is only one absinthe on the U.S. market using wormwood from this region: Vieux Pontarlier.

CHECKLIST

— FOR —

ABSINTHE

LABELS

☐ A minimum of 50 percent alcohol [100 proof]. The best historic absinthes were at least 65 percent [130 proof].

☐ No added sugar. Absinthe was always a "dry" spirit. If a product labels itself as a *liqueur/liquor*, it most likely will contain sugar.

☐ Look for the term *distilled*.

☐ The base alcohols of the best absinthes are grape/wine derived. Though modern grain or beet-neutral alcohol is perfectly acceptable for absinthe making, they have always been considered inferior.

☐ Avoid artificially colored absinthes, usually identified with an FD&C number, which has to be on the label if coloring is used. Switzerland does not allow absinthes to be artificially dyed, so you can be sure that any Swiss-made absinthe will be naturally colored.

ABSINTHE TOOLS AND ACCOUTREMENTS

Absinthe Spoons Absinthe spoons come in a variety of styles but most are ornate, lustrous, and look as if they were designed to kill vampires. Yet they are important tools that play an integral role in the creation and consumption of the perfectly concocted drink of absinthe.

Absinthe spoons are laid across the absinthe glass with the slotted portion centered in the middle so that when the ice cold water dissolves the sugar cubes, it drips directly into the glass. Most absinthe spoons have grooves in their stems that offer greater stability by clasping the glass's rim, while others rely on a completely flat architecture for a horizontal posture across the top. However, everything about an absinthe spoon's layout and style is carefully thought out by an experienced crafter with a particular vision, motif, person, or other source of inspiration in mind. There is an art to everything about absinthe.

Absinthe Glasses Absinthe glasses come in a variety of styles, and each offers absin-theurs a sweeping range of techniques and experiences. From simple elegance for beginners to sophisticated craftsmanship for veteran collectors, there is an absinthe glass for just about every drinking environment and inclination.

Obviously, absinthe glasses hold the absinthe that the ice cold sugar water is dripped into, but the important and differentiating factor is exactly *how* the glass holds the concoction. Remember, aesthetics are essential when consuming absinthe.

Many absinthe glasses have a demarcation line, called the dose line or mark line, that indicates exactly how much absinthe to pour into it. This frees drinkers from having to use jiggers or shot glasses and allows them to pour straight from the bottle. These markings typically ensure that the correct ratio of water to absinthe is achieved——anywhere from a 5:1 ratio to a 3:1 ratio depending on individual preferences. The dose line or mark line can also come in the form of a compartment referred to as a reservoir.

Accessories The following absinthe accessories are for absintheurs with an elevated level of enthusiasm for the beverage because——unlike absinthe spoons and glasses—— decanters, fountains, and pipes are not absolutely necessary for the absinthe ritual. They do intensify the absinthe experience by adding grace, eloquence, and sophistication to the process. Streaming ice water from a standard drinking glass exudes simplicity and a welcome lack of pretension; for serious absinthe drinkers, however, decanters, fountains, and pipes elevate the stakes by seriously considering every detail of consuming absinthe.

Decanters Decanters have been around since the dawn of ancient civilizations, but the modern glass varieties play an important role in absinthe consumption: on a practical level, the transparent glass allows pourers to measure the pace and proportion of ice water as it streams onto the disintegrating sugar cube, and on an artistic level they add a beautiful and more refined aesthetic to the ceremony.

Fountains Absinthe fountains are the ultimate centerpiece for the serious absinthe drinking ceremony. Absinthe fountains are beautiful, elaborate, fragile, sophisticated, and fun. No one walks away from an absinthe fountain. They are intriguing for novices and experts alike, and create the perfect atmosphere for absinthe parties because they require that people be close together while making their louches. Absinthe fountains are that conducive to the good life.

Like much of the absinthe experience, absinthe fountains are centered around the force of gravity. Fountains are made from metal stands, lids, and taps, usually silver or gold plated, and glass containers, which are available in various shapes——some of them quite exquisite and even sexy. Fountains are designed for entertaining. They typically have an even number of taps——four is most common——and are designed to engage groups of people in the absinthe drinking experience. The glass container is filled with ice and water, the lid is placed on the top to insulate the cold, and then, with a gentle turn of the knobs on the taps, a fine stream of ice cold water trickles out, much like from a miniature faucet. The cold water mixes with the absinthe in the glass below, and a louche steadily forms, creating the ideal drink of absinthe.

SIMPLE SYRUP

MAKES ABOUT **1½** CUPS

1 CUP **GRANULATED SUGAR**
1 CUP **WATER**

Combine the sugar and water in a small saucepan. Bring the mixture to a boil over moderately high heat; simmer for 3 minutes, stirring to dissolve the sugar. Allow to cool. Then transfer the syrup to a jar, cover it, and refrigerate until ready to use.

···

RICH SIMPLE SYRUP

Demerara sugar gives this concentrated syrup a great molasses flavor. The syrup keeps for up to a month in the fridge.

MAKES ABOUT **1** CUP

1 CUP **DEMERARA SUGAR**
½ CUP **WATER**

Combine the sugar and water in a small saucepan. Bring the mixture to a boil over moderately high heat; simmer for 3 minutes, stirring to dissolve the sugar. Allow to cool. Then transfer the syrup to a jar, cover it, and refrigerate until ready to use.

CHAPTER

1

· ABSINTHE ·

CLASSICS

∼ RECIPES ∼

The classic manner of drinking absinthe——known as the absinthe drip—— is drenched in ritual and technique, and necessitates the use of specially crafted vessels and serving pieces. The drip is also the most popular, simplest, and, according to true absintheurs, *only* way to prepare and drink the beverage. Fittingly, the traditional method exemplifies the social and intellectual experience that is part of its rich image and attraction. It's also a showcase of absinthe as it was enjoyed in the Belle period of the late nineteenth century on the streets of Paris, and in the cabarets of the red-light district in nearby Montmartre, home to the infamous Moulin Rouge.

The details of the traditional style complete the pleasure of the ritual——how to set up the glass and spoon, position the sugar, and monitor the ice cold water as it inter- acts with the elixir to create the opalescent louche. It doesn't require special ingredients or an experienced mixologist. The contemplative and methodical process of the tradi- tional-style recipe is about ritual, and requires both preparation and participation—— an excellent way to socialize and enjoy the company of your friends.

ABSINTHE DRIP

1½ OUNCES
**VIEUX PONTARLIER
ABSINTHE**

—✦—

1
SUGAR CUBE

—✦—

4½ TO 6 OUNCES
ICE COLD FILTERED WATER

*G*iven the high proof of traditional absinthe, it should never be consumed undiluted. Many purists agree that the traditional absinthe drip is the best way to appreciate the nuances of fine absinthe. Here is a version adapted from The Bar-Tenders Guide: How to Mix Drinks, or the Bon-Vivants Companion *by Jerry Thomas, which was published in* 1862.

Carefully pour the absinthe into an absinthe glass. Place a slotted absinthe spoon over the rim of the glass and set a sugar cube in the bowl of the spoon. [If you don't want your absinthe sweetened, omit the spoon and sugar cube.] Slowly pour or drip the ice cold water over the sugar cube and into the absinthe. As the dripping water dissolves the sugar cube, watch the layer of undiluted absinthe rise to the top of the glass. When the mixture is completely cloudy, the drink should be ready. Stir, taste for strength, and adjust with more water if necessary.

CORPSE REVIVER №2

¾ OUNCE
MARTIN MILLERS GIN

¾ OUNCE
COINTREAU

¾ OUNCE
LILLET BLANC

¾ OUNCE
LEMON JUICE

4 DROPS
ABSINTHE

*T*his is an adaptation of one of the two "corpse revivers" listed in the venerable Savoy Cocktail Book [1930] *and attributed to Harry Craddock. Historians believe corpse revivers were morning drinks, probably prescribed by bartenders, relied upon to revive and ameliorate symptoms most likely stemming from the previous night's tipple. Marcos Tello adapted the recipe for the Edison in downtown Los Angeles.*

Pour the gin, Cointreau, Lillet, and lemon juice into a mixing glass, then add ice. Shake well and strain the drink into a chilled coupe. Add the absinthe and serve.

COCKTAIL À LA LOUISIANE

2 OUNCES
**WILD TURKEY
RYE WHISKEY**

¾ OUNCE
DOLIN SWEET VERMOUTH

¾ OUNCE
BENEDICTINE

3 DASHES
EDOUARD ABSINTHE

3 DASHES
PEYCHAUD'S BITTERS

**3
BRANDIED CHERRIES,**
for garnish

*A*ccording to author Stanley Arthur Clisby in his book Famous New Orleans Drinks and How to Mix 'Em [1937], *"This is the special cocktail served at restaurant Restaurant de la Louisiane, one of the famous French restaurants of New Orleans, long the rendezvous of those who appreciate the best in creole cusine."* The strong presence of French culture in New Orleans cuisine and beverages still lingers in the city's affection for absinthe-based flavors. Jim Meehan of PDT, a modern-day speakeasy and hidden gem in New York City's East Village, developed this recipe at Pace, an Italian restaurant where he served as bar manager and sommelier.

Pour the whiskey, vermouth, Benedictine, absinthe, and bitters into a mixing glass, then add ice. Stir well and strain the drink into a chilled coupe with one large ice cube in it. Garnish with three brandied cherries on a cocktail pick. Serve.

A SALUTE TO THE
SAZERAC

VIEUX PONTARLIER,
for rinsing the glass

1
DEMERARA SUGAR CUBE

3 DASHES
PEYCHAUD'S BITTERS

2 OUNCES
**RITTENHOUSE
RYE WHISKEY**

LEMON PEEL

*A*ward-winning bartender Jim Meehan reworked this famous New Orleans classic for PDT, the cocktail lounge in New York City's East Village [pictured opposite], of which Jim is a managing partner. Most likely named after a defunct brand of Cognac named Sazerac de Forge et Fils, this drink nowadays most commonly uses rye whiskey as the base. Cognac was likely the preferred ingredient in the nineteenth century.

Rinse a chilled old-fashioned glass with Vieux Pontarlier; set aside.

Muddle the sugar cube and bitters in a mixing glass. Add rye and fill the cocktail shaker with ice. Stir well and strain the drink into the prepared old-fashioned glass. Twist a lemon peel over the surface of the drink to release its oils, and discard the peel. Serve.

ARSENIC AND OLD LACE

ABSINTHE,
for rinsing the glass

—❧—

2 OUNCES
GIN

—❧—

¾ OUNCE
DRY VERMOUTH

—❧—

¼ OUNCE
CRÈME DE VIOLETTE

—❧—

THIN SLICE OF
ORANGE PEEL,
for garnish

*A*aron Polsky at White Star, New York City, found inspiration in a recipe from Cocktail Guide and Ladies' Companion by Crosby Gaige when creating this cocktail. The presence of crème de violette adds a floral and sweet influence that tempers the harsher gin and dry vermouth qualities.

IN THE 1966 FILM *Madame X*, director David Lowell Rich utilizes absinthe as an emotional crutch for the main character, played by Lana Turner. The film entails a complicated plot about a woman, known only as Madame X, standing trial for murder who refuses to give her own name in order to protect the socialite status of her husband and son. Madame X uses absinthe to try to drown her sorrows of losing her husband, home, and baby son in the name of that all-important thing: reputation.

Rinse a chilled cocktail glass with absinthe; set aside.

Fill a mixing glass with freshly cracked ice. Add the gin, vermouth, and crème de violette, and stir well. Strain the drink into the prepared cocktail glass. Squeeze the orange peel over the top, and drop the peel into the glass. Serve.

ABSINTHE AND OLD LACE

1
EGG WHITE

1 OUNCE
BEEFEATER GIN

½ OUNCE
PERNOD ABSINTHE

½ OUNCE
GREEN CRÈME DE MENTHE

½ OUNCE
SIMPLE SYRUP
[*page 24*]

½ OUNCE
CREAM

1 DASH
BITTERMENS XOCOLOTL MOLE BITTERS

The name of this cocktail was inspired by the classic play and film of the same name. From Jackson Cannon of Eastern Standard, in Boston, it's a fine example of how absinthe can add depth and complexity to an after-dinner drink.

Pour the egg white, gin, absinthe, crème de menthe, simple syrup, cream, and bitters into a mixing glass. Dry shake well, then add ice and shake again. Strain the drink into a chilled cocktail glass. Serve.

IN 1956, director Vincente Minnelli featured absinthe in *Lust for Life*, a biographical film adapted from the 1934 novel by Irving Stone. The story follows the tumultuous life of the Dutch painter Vincent van Gogh, played by Kirk Douglas, and absinthe has a large role. Popular mythology claims van Gogh chopped off his own ear as a result of absinthe's influence.

BRUNELLE

1½ OUNCES
LEMON JUICE

½ OUNCE
ABSINTHE

1½ TEASPOONS
SUGAR

I tried this cocktail——from the 1930 Savoy cocktail book——before the ban on absinthe was lifted, when all I had to work with was pastis. The cocktail was good but not outstanding. After the ban, I decided to try it again with the real stuff. Wow! Now this is one of my favorite drinks. It reminds me of the wonderful aroma when you hike through the chaparral at Big Sur. The recipe here is further refined by Tim Stookey of San Francisco's Presidio Social Club.

THE HENROID SISTERS who bought Dr. Ordinaire's original recipe for absinthe reportedly sold it to Major Dubied in 1797. Some years later, the major, his son, and his son-in-law, Henri-Louis Pernod, opened the first commercial absinthe distillery, which they named Dubied Père et Fils. When they moved the business to a larger location, they renamed it Maison Pernod Fils. Their eponymous absinthe is still one of the best on the market.

Pour the lemon juice, absinthe, and sugar into a cocktail shaker filled with ice. Shake well, and strain the drink into a cocktail glass. Serve.

PAN AMERICAN CLIPPER

2 OUNCES
DOMAINE DE MONTREUIL CALVADOS

½ OUNCE
FRESH LIME JUICE

½ OUNCE
SMALL HAND FOODS GRENADINE

3 DASHES
DUPLAIS ABSINTHE

LIME TWIST

*O*riginally printed in The Gentlemen's Companion by Charles H. Baker in 1939, this recipe was adapted by Erik Adkins for the menu of San Francisco's Heaven's Dog to feature a more contemporary flavor.

ABSINTHE is the spelling most commonly used for Swiss and French products. The Spanish label their bottles as *absenta*, and the Germans prefer to use the spelling *absinth*.

Pour the calvados, lime juice, grenadine, and absinthe into a cocktail shaker. Add ice and shake for 10 to 20 seconds, or until cold. Strain the drink into a coupe. Garnish with a lime twist, and serve.

IMPROVED
POLSKI POUSSE CAFÉ

¼ OUNCE
YELLOW CHARTREUSE

1
SMALL EGG YOLK

½ OUNCE
DANTZIGER GOLDWASSER

DASH
ABSINTHE

A classic cocktail adapted from Charles H. Baker's book The Gentlemen's Companion, *pousse café* translates to "coffee push." This sweet, boozy, layered drink was intended to be taken after your coffee. The original Polski Pousse Café did not call for absinthe, but this version by Jason "Buffalo" Lograsso of Bourbon & Branch, San Francisco, uses absinthe as the final touch.

Slowly pour the chartreuse over the back of a spoon into a sherry glass. Repeat with the egg yolk and then the Dantziger Goldwasser, carefully layering each ingredient on top of the previous one. Add a dash of absinthe and serve.

MONKEY GLAND

1½ OUNCES
MILLER'S GIN

1½ OUNCES
ORANGE JUICE

1 BARSPOON
POMEGRANATE GRENADINE

6 DROPS
PERNOD ABSINTHE

1
MARASCHINO CHERRY

STRIP OF
ORANGE ZEST

*T*his cocktail was invented by Harry MacElhone in the 1920s at Harry's New York Bar in Paris, France. The recipe here is from Jackson Cannon at Eastern Standard, Boston. Its unusual name comes from an equally unusual practice at the time of surgically implanting a monkey's testicle into men to give them "renewed vigor." Frankly, I think drinking this cocktail would have more effect and the monkeys would appreciate it as well!

Pour the gin, orange juice, grenadine, and absinthe into a cocktail shaker. Add ice, and shake well. Strain the drink into a chilled cocktail glass.

Make a "petit flag" garnish by spearing the cherry onto a cocktail pick and wrapping the orange twist around the cherry. Add to the glass, and serve.

MONKEY GLAND №2

1¾ OUNCES
GIN

—◦◦◦—

¾ OUNCE
ORANGE JUICE

—◦◦◦—

¼ OUNCE
GRENADINE

—◦◦◦—

⅛ OUNCE
ABSINTHE BLANCHE

John Gersten of Drink in Boston, Massachusetts, added his own spin to the venerable Monkey Gland recipes by altering the proportions and types of ingredients and excluding the cherry flavor.

OTHER FLAVORING ingredients used in absinthe include: roman wormwood, star anise, anise seed, hyssop, angelica root, calamis root, fennel, melissa, juniper, nutmeg, coriander, licorice root, lemon balm, dittany, and sweet flag.

Pour the gin, orange juice, grenadine, and absinthe into an iced cocktail shaker. Shake well, and strain the drink into a cocktail glass. Serve.

DEATH ·IN· THE AFTERNOON

½ OUNCE
ABSINTHE VERTE

CHAMPAGNE

This refreshing beverage incorporates the subtle qualities of absinthe verte with the more effervescent texture and fizz of Champagne. Thank John Gersten of Boston's Drink for developing another simple but inspired cocktail perfect for absinthe fans with reason to celebrate.

BURNING THE ABSINTHE-SOAKED SUGAR CUBE before drinking the beverage is a relatively new invention and not part of the original ritual. Absinthe purists denounce the practice.

Pour the absinthe into a champagne flute. Fill the glass to the top with Champagne. Serve.

"B" MONKEY

*M*arc Hartenfels of Bardessono in Napa Valley, California, explains that the "b" monkey is their version of the Monkey Gland, which was invented by Harry MacElhone, owner of Harry's New York Bar in Paris, in the 1920s. Hartenfels has created his own version of the conventional Monkey Gland recipe by replacing the orange flavor with grapefruit. Also, no cherry.

1½ OUNCES	**1 TABLESPOON**
LEOPOLD'S GIN	**ST. GEORGE ABSINTHE**
1½ OUNCES	**1 TABLESPOON**
FRESH GRAPEFRUIT JUICE	**GRENADINE**

Pour the gin, grapefruit juice, absinthe, and grenadine into a cocktail shaker. Add ice and shake well. Strain into a small cocktail glass. Serve.

. A MOMENT IN .

ABSINTHE
History

The story of absinthe——the most vilified beverage in history——begins in 1797 with Dr. Pierre Ordinaire, a Frenchman who dedicated his life to helping people with their ailments. Unfortunately, addressing medical needs during this time period often meant not curing but numbing distress. Over time, Dr. Ordinaire's search to relieve his patients from pain would lead to what would be creepy-eyed shock rocker Marilyn Manson's favorite beverage.

Though the liquor's history is poorly comprehended and surrounded by innuendo and apocryphal tales of grimness and grandeur, all accounts point to Dr. Ordinaire as the father of the Green Fairy. In 1789, the doctor practiced medicine in Val-de-Travers in the Canton of Neuchâtel, a region of Switzerland near the French border. Wanting to mollify his patients of their anguish and disease, he sought remedies from all aspects of his life, and especially from the various natural plants that grew around his home. By tinkering with the herb *Artemisia absinthium*, Dr. Ordinaire concocted a beverage that millions would struggle to understand throughout the next two centuries. His cure-all, absinthe, was made from the leaves and flowers of wormwood, a plant named as if it belonged in a witch's cauldron, steaming alongside puppy whiskers and butterfly wings. Originally administered by the spoonful as any ordinary cough medicine, the elixir curiously made its way into the barkeep's cabinet to become one of the most fascinating beverages of all time.

CHAPTER

2

FRUIT &

CITRUS

⹀ RECIPES ⹀

Absinthe's reputation is steeped in a dark and gothic history where artists and intellectuals consumed the drink on lonely benders in dark rooms filled with torn canvases and crumpled pages of wayward manuscripts. However, with absinthe's resurrection comes a newfound understanding of the drink, one that allows the Green Fairy to fly freely about the limitless range of mixers and ingredients available to complement absinthe's distinctive flavor——including a taste of the tropics. There is no reason absinthe should remain cloistered in its brooding history and kept out of the sunlight. So here are some tropical recipes that feature citrus flavors and influences reminiscent of palm trees, bright colors, and balmy weather.

BITTER END

*T*hough carrying unhappy connotations, the name of this cocktail——created by Josh Harris, cofounder of the Bon Vivantes in San Francisco——comes from its citrus flavors. It's a small drink and perfect as an aperitif to whet the appetite. The fun thing about this drink is that the taste at the beginning is different from the taste at the end. It starts out sweet, tart, citrusy, and then, as you get to the bottom, the drink becomes more aggressively bitter. The Campari has a real nice bite to it.

½ OUNCE
FRESH LEMON JUICE

½ OUNCE
FRESH ORANGE JUICE

½ OUNCE
FRESH EGG WHITE

1 OUNCE
KÜBLER ABSINTHE

½ OUNCE
COINTREAU

¼ OUNCE
RICH SIMPLE SYRUP
[page 24]

¼ OUNCE
CAMPARI

STAR ANISE POD,
for garnish

Pour the lemon juice, orange juice, and egg white into a cocktail shaker. Using a blender ball, dry shake the mixture until well combined. Open the shaker, and then pour in the absinthe, Cointreau, and simple syrup. Shake again, vigorously, and then strain into a martini glass. Slowly and carefully, pour the Campari down the side of the glass so that it sinks below the absinthe mixture [this is easier to do if you fit your Campari bottle with a medium-flow long chrome pour spout]. Garnish by floating the star anise pod on top of the drink, and serve.

LA FISCUS VERTE

3
MISSION FIGS,
halved

1 TEASPOON
FRESH LEMON JUICE

DASH
**TAHITIAN VANILLA BEAN
SIMPLE SYRUP**

1 SLICE
VALENCIA ORANGE

3 OUNCES
LEBLON CACHAÇA

SPLASH
ABSINTHE VERTE

3 DASHES
BITTERS

ORANGE TWIST,
for garnish

*T*he name of this cocktail is a combination of the Latin words for "the green fig" and the French for absinthe's nickname, the Green Fairy, *la fee verte. Creator Paul Scandura of Martini House in Napa Valley, California, wanted the name in Latin to represent the rich history of absinthe and how it is commonly referred to in historical literature. You can find the Tahitian vanilla bean syrup in specialty grocery stores or some coffee shops.*

Muddle the figs, lemon juice, vanilla syrup, and orange slice in a cocktail shaker. Top the mixing glass with ice, then add the cachaça and absinthe. Shake all ingredients together and strain into chilled martini glass. Add the bitters, garnish with twist of orange, and serve.

THE STRUTTERS' BALL

*T*he "Strutters' Ball," the secondary name for the song more commonly know as "Caliope," can often be heard on the steam piano of the Natchez steamboat, which docks on the Mississippi River in New Orleans. Jason "Buffalo" Lograsso of Bourbon & Branch in San Francisco was inspired to make this cocktail by his memory of sipping a sweet, milky Cafe du Monde iced coffee by the riverside on his first morning in New Orleans. His personal experience is revisited in this cocktail via the influences of the sweetened condensed milk.

2 OUNCES
SAGATIBA VELHA CACHAÇA

—❦—

1 OUNCE
SWEETENED CONDENSED MILK

—❦—

1½ OUNCES
FRESH GRAPEFRUIT JUICE

—❦—

1 OUNCE
FRESH ORANGE JUICE

½ OUNCE
FRESH LIME JUICE

—❦—

¼ OUNCE
ABSINTHE

—❦—

COCOA NIBS,
for garnish

—❦—

1 THIN SLICE OF ORANGE,
for garnish

—❦—

STAR ANISE,
for garnish

Pour the cachaça, sweetened condensed milk, grapefruit juice, orange juice, lime juice, and absinthe into a cocktail shaker. Shake well, and strain the drink into a highball glass filled with ice. Garnish with the cocoa nibs, orange slice, and star anise. Serve.

BLUE RHONE FIZZ

*I*nspired by a love for fresh, organic ingredients and original recipes, this drink features the expertise of Scott Baird, of 15 Romolo and the Bon Vivants in San Francisco. Baird, a lover of art in many forms, has worked in jobs as diverse as florist, caterer, window display designer, and welder. That versatile background and courage to try new things are evident in this blueberry-influenced cocktail.

2 OUNCES
BLUEBERRY-INFUSED GIN
[SEE RECIPE BELOW]

½ OUNCE
VIEUX PONTARLIER ABSINTHE

1 OUNCE **LEMON JUICE**

¾ OUNCE
RICH SIMPLE SYRUP
[*page* 24]

½ OUNCE **CREAM**

1 OUNCE **EGG WHITE**

1 DASH
ANGOSTURA ORANGE BITTERS

1½ OUNCES
SELTZER

4 DROPS **ROSEWATER**

BLUEBERRIES, FOR GARNISH

WIDE STRIP OF
LEMON ZEST, FOR GARNISH

Add the gin, absinthe, lemon juice, simple syrup, cream, egg white, and bitters to a pint glass. Dry shake using a Hawthorn strainer for 30 seconds. Add ice and shake hard.

Pour the seltzer into a Collins glass, then strain the cocktail into the glass. Garnish with rosewater and a blueberry-lemon skewer, and serve.

BLUEBERRY-
INFUSED GIN

1 CUP **FRESH BLUEBERRIES**

6 TABLESPOONS **SUGAR**

750 ML **GIN**

Place the blueberries in a large glass bottle, and then add the sugar and gin. Shake well. Allow the mixture to infuse for at least two weeks or up to two months maximum, making sure to shake the bottle occasionally, until the mixture turns a deep blue color.

NORTH · OF · THE · BORDER

½ OUNCE
SIMPLE SYRUP
[page 24]

½ OUNCE
FRESH LEMON JUICE

½ OUNCE
FRESH ORANGE JUICE

½ OUNCE
ABSINTHE

2 OUNCES
CROWN ROYAL WHISKY

ANGOSTURA BITTERS

*V*ery north of the border, indeed, this cocktail was born from the style of New York City bartenders Shane Tison and Jason Littrell, who work at the Randolph at Broome in downtown Manhattan. The lemon and orange citrus influences blend well with the Crown Royal, a Canadian whisky much loved and consumed by Canada's southern neighbors.

Pour the simple syrup, lemon juice, orange juice, absinthe, and whisky into a cocktail shaker. Shake well, and pour the drink into a Collins glass filled with crushed ice. Add two dashes of bitters, and serve.

QUINQUINA

1 OUNCE
COGNAC

1 OUNCE
LILLET BLANC

1 OUNCE
**PEACH BRANDY
LIQUEUR**

¼ OUNCE
ABSINTHE

Quinquina are a type of bitters that have quinine as a key flavoring. The quinine is the bitter constituent which promotes production of digestive enzymes and, therefore, appetite. One of the most popular and widely known quinquinas is Lillet Blanc; before 1986, when the recipe was modified to make it lighter and less bitter, it was sold as Kina Lillet. Lillet is the quinine element in this classic cocktail from Eric Alperin of The Varnish in Los Angeles. If you like the taste of bitter aperitifs, you should enjoy this heftier peach-and-anise-laced version of a Quinquina cocktail.

Pour the cognac, Lillet Blanc, liqueur, and absinthe into a cocktail shaker. Shake vigorously, and strain into a chilled coupe. Serve.

L'ARC DE TRIOMPHE

1 OUNCE
ABSINTHE

1 OUNCE
FRESH ORANGE JUICE

1 OUNCE
FRESH LEMON JUICE

1 OUNCE
BITTER ORANGE MARMALADE

¾ OUNCE
EGG WHITE

PEYCHAUD'S BITTERS

1 OUNCE
SELTZER

WIDE STRIP OF
ORANGE ZEST,
for garnish

*F*eaturing the unique influence of bitter orange marmalade, this cocktail from Scott Baird of 15 Romolo and the Bon Vivants in San Francisco is a bold and colorful quaff. Scott particularly enjoys drinking this recipe in the afternoon because it's a good, long drink that is not terribly alcoholic——a perfect afternoon cocktail.

Add the absinthe, orange juice, lemon juice, marmalade, egg white, and a dash of Peychaud's to a pint glass with the spring from a Hawthorn strainer [remove the spring from the strainer and drop it in the glass]. Dry shake for 30 seconds, until it is nice and frothy. Open it up, add ice, and shake well to make cold.

Pour the seltzer into a footed beer glass or short-stemmed wineglass. Strain the drink into the glass. Add 2 dashes of Peychaud's and garnish with orange zest. Serve.

DR. FUNK

½ LIME

—❧—

1½ OUNCES
RHUM AGRICOLE BLANC

—❧—

½ OUNCE
FRESH LEMON JUICE

—❧—

½ OUNCE
GRENADINE

—❧—

¼ OUNCE
ABSINTHE BLANCHE

—❧—

SODA WATER

*D*rink's *John Gersten*——voted "Best Bartender" by Boston Magazine *in 2008*——concocted this drink that features a French-Caribbean-made sugarcane-based liquor. You don't need to have a sweet tooth to enjoy this drink, just a taste for the Caribbean.

IN THE 1978 FILM *Pretty Baby,* absinthe is used in the hedonistic lifestyle of 1917 New Orleans' Red Light District, where the story follows Violet, a twelve-year-old girl——played by Brooke Shields——living in a brothel full of other young girls like herself.

Squeeze the juice from the lime into a cocktail shaker, and add the lime. Pour in the rum, lemon juice, grenadine, and absinthe, and top with ice. Shake well and strain the drink into a highball glass filled with crushed ice. Top off the drink with soda, and serve.

ICEBERG

1 OUNCE
KÜBLER ABSINTHE

—❦—

1 OUNCE
YELLOW CHARTREUSE

—❦—

¾ OUNCE
FRESH LIME JUICE

—❦—

½ OUNCE
SIMPLE SYRUP
[*page* 24]

—❦—

LIME ZEST

Calling specifically for Kübler absinthe, this cocktail is by Mae Lane, who is not only a mixologist at Griffou in New York City but also a country music singer who loves the 1940s and dresses accordingly. Her unique personality is poured into this recipe, which features the bold taste of lime with the more temperate and sweeter flavor and aroma of yellow chartreuse.

Total Eclipse, **A FILM FROM 1995**, tells a dark story that takes place in the early 1870s, following the absinthe-heated and passionate affair between Paul Verlaine, played by David Thewlis, and teenage French poet Arthur Rimbaud, played by Leonardo DiCaprio. The intensity of their relationship erupted into a fiery argument in which Verlaine shot Rimbaud in the hand——this incident effected the end of Rimbaud's career as a poet.

Pour the absinthe, yellow chartreuse, lime juice, and simple syrup into a hurricane glass. Add a pinch of lime zest, and fill the glass with crushed ice. Garnish with lime zest, and serve.

DEV'S PRIDE

1 OUNCE
FRESH ORANGE JUICE

3
STRAWBERRIES

1 OUNCE
St. GERMAIN
ELDERFLOWER LIQUEUR

1 OUNCE
ABSINTHE

¾ OUNCE
CREAM

*T*his strawberry drink comes to us from Hari Nathan Kalyan, owner of the Randolph at Broome in New York City. The combination of fruits complements the herbal notes of absinthe.

MARILYN MANSON developed his own brand of absinthe, Mansinthe, which has an alcohol content of 66.6 percent.

Put the orange juice and 2 strawberries in a cocktail shaker, and muddle together. Add the liqueur, absinthe, and cream. Shake well, and strain the drink into a coupe. Garnish with the remaining strawberry, and serve.

GRAND TI PUNCH

2 OUNCES
**RHUM CLÉMENT
PREMIÈRE CANNE**

½ OUNCE
SIMPLE SYRUP
[*page 24*]

¼ OUNCE
ABSINTHE

1 SMALL SLICE OF
LIME

*N*eyah White of San Francisco's Nopa thinks this is probably the most traditional way to drink rhum agricole——a spirit made from fresh pressed sugarcane from the French Caribbean. The word ti is a diminutive of petite, in French, so this drink is a "big little punch."

Pour the rhum, simple syrup, and absinthe into a tumbler with a few pieces of ice, and stir. Garnish with the lime slice, and serve.

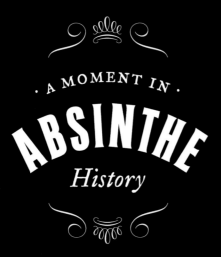

A MOMENT IN

ABSINTHE

History

At the turn of the twentieth century, the detractors of absinthe began to organize. By the time the liquor had reached new heights in popularity in the districts of Paris, so had the international temperance movement to abolish drunkenness. The movement——starting as far back as the 1820s——was well organized with medical professionals, political associations, and committees throughout England, Scotland, Canada, Africa, India, and the United States. In 1854, *The Pathology of Drunkenness* by Charles Wilson, MD, of Edinburgh, Scotland, furthered the temperance movement's cause, claiming that drunkenness was a deliberate attempt to commit suicide. Reports and recommendations similar to this book were published claiming that alcohol served no purpose for medical use or pleasure, and the only way to stop drunkenness was to embrace total abstinence. As early as 1870, rival manufactures of other spirits joined the bandwagon to demonize the Green Fairy. The only missing piece of the social engineering puzzle was a violent, high-profile, attention-grabbing murder case to support their beliefs and condemn the beverage.

Enter Swiss farmer Jean Lanfray, who——after drinking absinthe, among other spirits——murdered his wife and daughters. The press deemed the crime the "Absinthe Murders." During the trial, a psychologist testified that a "classic case of absinthe madness" had overwhelmed Lanfray. The public was outraged. By 1910, absinthe was banned in Switzerland. The rest of the world soon followed.

THAI HALLUCINATION

1 OUNCE
ST. GERMAIN ELDERFLOWER LIQUEUR

1 OUNCE
ABSINTHE

1 OUNCE
FRESH LEMON JUICE

GUAVA SODA

ORANGE PEEL

This offering from Jason Littrell of the Randolph at Broome features a unique splash of guava soda. You should think of the beach when you think of this drink. That light tartness of the lemon balances the fullness of the guava, and the unique woody flavor of the absinthe will come out underneath the tropical flavors.

Pour the liqueur, absinthe, and fresh lemon juice into a cocktail shaker, and shake well. Strain the drink into a Collins glass filled with ice. Top the cocktail with guava soda and garnish with the orange peel. Serve.

ZOMBIE PUNCH

*T*his is a classic tiki cocktail created by Donn the Beachcomber, the acknowledged founder of tiki bars, nightclubs, and restaurants, in 1934. Because of the Zombie's potent mix, he tried to limit each customer to one, stating that two will turn you into one. Brian Miller of Death + Company in New York City decided to re-create it after his friend Jeff "Beachbum" Berry said in a New York Times article that he could not get a decent one in Manhattan. When making this at home, you will need to make Donn's Mix the night before.

1½ OUNCES
AGED JAMAICAN RUM

1½ OUNCES
GOLD PUERTO RICAN RUM

1 OUNCE
DEMERARA 151 PROOF RUM

¾ OUNCE
FRESH LIME JUICE

½ OUNCE
DONN'S MIX
[SEE RECIPE BELOW]

½ OUNCE
VELVET FALERNUM

1 TEASPOON
GRENADINE

⅛ TEASPOON
VIEUX PONTARLIER ABSINTHE

1 DASH
ANGOSTURA BITTERS

MINT SPRIG,
for garnish

Pour the rums, lime juice, Donn's Mix, falernum, grenadine, absinthe, and a dash of bitters into a cocktail shaker. Add 3 ice cubes and shake well. Strain the drink into a tiki mug filled with crushed ice. Garnish with the mint sprig, and serve.

DONN'S MIX

MAKES **4½** CUPS

3 CINNAMON STICKS

1 CUP **SUGAR**

Crush the cinnamon sticks in a saucepan. Add the sugar and 1 cup of water, place the pan over medium-high heat, stir, and bring to a boil. Reduce the heat to low and simmer, covered, for 3 minutes. Remove the saucepan from the heat and let stand, still covered, overnight. Then strain into an airtight container and refrigerate up to 3 weeks.

MY OH MY TY

*T*his cocktail is an ode to the tiki classic by Trader Vic. Brian Miller, of Death + Company in
New York City, named this drink after his good friend Ty Baker, who was the commis-
sioner of the Papa Doble "Beard-Off" best beard competition held at Death + Company in 2008.
Although Miller was hoping to curry favor with Baker and the rest of the judges, it didn't do the
trick. As much as they loved the drink, Miller and his beard finished third.

1 OUNCE **FRESH LIME JUICE**	**½** OUNCE **PREMIER ESSENCE** **ORGEAT**	**1** OUNCE **LA FAVORITE** **BLANC RHUM**
⅛ OUNCE **SIMPLE SYRUP** [*page 24*]	**¼** OUNCE **VIEUX PONTARLIER** **ABSINTHE**	**1** OUNCE **FLOR DE CAÑA** **7 YEAR RUM**
½ OUNCE **RHUM CLÉMENT CRÉOLE** **SHRUBB LIQUEUR**		SPRIG OF **MINT,** *for garnish*

Pour the lime juice, simple syrup, liqueur, orgeat essence, absinthe, and rums into a
cocktail shaker. Add 3 ice cubes. Shake well and strain the drink into a coconut mug filled
with crushed ice. Garnish with the mint sprig, and serve.

SUISSESSE

1 OUNCE
ABSINTHE BLANCHE

⁓❦⁓

½ OUNCE
ANISETTE

⁓❦⁓

SODA WATER

A simple recipe, this cocktail by John Gersten of Drink in Boston highlights how well absinthe mixes with anisette.

LA BLEUE absinthe was a product made by bootleggers in the mountains of Switzerland.

Pour the absinthe and anisette into a cocktail shaker filled with crushed ice. Shake well and strain the drink into a highball glass filled with ice. Top with soda water, and serve.

CHAPTER

3

·WHISKEY &·

GIN

RECIPES

Americans love their whiskey and gin, and just as these two spirits have experienced a love/hate relationship with the American public——their own legends and lore part of the unique history of the United States——both whiskey and gin happen to make great companions with a drink as storied and complex as absinthe.

In fact, the pairing of absinthe with whiskey and gin marks a crossroads for the Green Fairy, as it heralds a level of acceptance not witnessed before by absinthe enthusiasts. As Americans become more accustomed to absinthe, it will increasingly become more prevalent in cultural events and on bar shelves, where gin and whiskey have been promoted throughout history.

LAST SECOND

2 OUNCES
BOLS GENEVER

—⊱⊰—

½ OUNCE
**VIEUX PONTARLIER
ABSINTHE**

—⊱⊰—

½ OUNCE
APRICOT BRANDY

—⊱⊰—

1 DASH
MINT BITTERS

*T*his cocktail by Jeff Hollinger of Absinthe Brasserie & Bar in San Francisco combines a variety of flavors including the malt flavor in Bols Genever, the herbal taste and aroma of Vieux Pontarlier absinthe, apricot brandy, and hint of mint bitter, an ingredient linking this cocktail to the popular mint julep and mojito.

Pour the Bols Genever, Vieux Pontarlier absinthe, and apricot brandy into a cocktail shaker filled with ice, and add a dash of mint bitters. Stir for 20 to 30 seconds or until the drink is well chilled. Strain the drink into a chilled port glass, and serve.

THE HOBNOB

*H*obnob *is an archaic word that means "to drink socially." A hob is also a mischievous fairy, playing on the idea of absinthe as the Green Fairy. Jonathan Henson of Press Restaurant in Napa Valley, California, added grapefruit zest and lime zest to this recipe because they not only add a flavorful citrus note but also work to enhance the flavors of the absinthe. The mixture of the grapefruit zest and absinthe creates a gentle numbing sensation on the tongue. To enhance this effect, trying infusing the gin ahead of time with the zest of a grapefruit.*

¼ OUNCE
ABSINTHE

ONE 1-INCH SQUARE OF
GRAPEFRUIT ZEST

ONE 1-INCH SQUARE OF
LIME ZEST

½ OUNCE
SIMPLE SYRUP
[*page* 24]

½ OUNCE
FRESH GRAPEFRUIT JUICE

½ OUNCE
FRESH LIME

2 OUNCES
NO. 209 GIN

½ OUNCE
**LUXARDO MARASCHINO
LIQUEUR**

STRIP OF
GRAPEFRUIT RIND,
for garnish

Pour the absinthe into an empty rocks glass. Wash the glass with absinthe and pour out the excess. Set glass aside.

Add grapefruit zest, lime zest, and simple syrup to a cocktail shaker. Muddle the zests until they begin to break apart. Add the grapefruit juice and lime juice. Fill the shaker with ice. Add the gin and maraschino liqueur. Shake hard. Strain the drink into the prepared glass. Garnish with a twist of grapefruit, and serve.

THE 1997 FILM *Wilde* depicts the story of Oscar Wilde, the genius poet and playwright. He was famed for his love of absinthe, once saying, "The first stage is like ordinary drinking, the second when you begin to see monstrous and cruel things, but if you can persevere you will enter in upon the third stage where you will see things that you will want to see, wonderful curious things."

BLACK FAIRY

4
FRESH BLACKBERRIES

—ᙏ—

FRESH MINT SPRIGS

—ᙏ—

¾ OUNCE
KÜBLER ABSINTHE

—ᙏ—

¾ OUNCE
MICHTER'S RYE WHISKEY

—ᙏ—

¾ OUNCE
FRESH LEMON JUICE

—ᙏ—

¾ OUNCE
FEVER TREE TONIC WATER

*T*he creator of this cocktail——Erika Fey of Cyrus in Healdsburg, California——frequently draws inspiration from the bounty of spectacular seasonal ingredients available from local Sonoma County farms to create unique cocktails with playful and surprising flavor combinations.

WHEN STORING ABSINTHE, treat it as you would a bottle of wine. Keep it in a cool place, with a consistent temperature, and make sure it is out of direct sunlight. Also, any bottle with a cork should be stored on its side so that the cork does not dry out.

In a cocktail shaker, muddle 3 of the blackberries with a mint sprig. Add the absinthe, rye whiskey, lemon juice, and tonic water. Fill the shaker with ice, and shake well. Strain the drink over an old-fashioned glass filled with fresh ice. Garnish with the remaining blackberry and a sprig of mint, and serve.

BOTTEGA'S
ABSINTHE MARTINI

½ OUNCE
ST. GEORGE ABSINTHE

2 OUNCES
BOMBAY SAPPHIRE GIN

½ OUNCE
GRAND MARNIER

ORANGE PEEL,
for garnish

*D*espite having a degree in exercise science, Melissa Sheppard of Bottega in Napa Valley, California, discovered her true passion in life was for mixing drinks, which she has been doing for more than eight years. This delicious cocktail demonstrates that she made the right decision. If you'd like a fancier presentation, coat the rim of the glass with sugar.

Pour the absinthe into a chilled martini glass. Swirl to coat, then discard the remaining absinthe.

Pour the gin and Grand Marnier into a cocktail shaker filled with ice. Shake well, and strain the drink into a martini glass. Garnish with orange peel, and serve.

OBITUARY

2¼ OUNCES
GIN

—◆—

½ OUNCE
DRY VERMOUTH

—◆—

¼ OUNCE
ABSINTHE

John Gersten from Drink in Boston recommends this cocktail he first enjoyed at the Lafite Blacksmith shop in the French Quarter of New Orleans. It's a very simple, old-school drink similar to a martini but with a fair amount of absinthe. It has a glow to it——not a "full-on louche," but a nice clarity——and makes an excellent predinner drink, crisp and refreshing. The Obituary is a little more appropriate for warm weather because of the lightness of the drink, but John wouldn't dissuade anyone from ordering it at any time of the year.

Pour the gin, vermouth, and absinthe into a chilled cocktail shaker, and stir to combine. Strain the drink into a cocktail glass, and serve.

· A MOMENT IN ·

ABSINTHE

History

Following the "Absinthe Murders," newspapers released numerous editorials and cartoons that vilified absinthe by depicting morose skeletons dancing with bottles, bleary-eyed men sucking their thumbs in insane asylums, and haggard drunkards lining the streets with only their wicked bottles of absinthe to keep them warm. The media blitz destroyed absinthe's reputation and led French authorities to eventually ban the drink. The war against absinthe reached a pinnacle in Switzerland on July 5, 1908, when Article 32 was added to their federal constitution banning all absinthes in the nation. The law went into effect on October 7, 1910. Though the Swiss were not the first to ban absinthe, the new legislation would prove to be a significant victory for the temperance movement in stopping absinthe production, considering that Switzerland represented one of the largest demographics of absinthe drinkers in Europe, second only to France.

By 1910, the consumption of absinthe in France had reached staggering levels. The liquor infiltrated every level of society, while alcoholism and drunkenness swept across the country. The French absinthe industry tried in vain to educate consumers on the truths of absinthe. The temperance groups, however, were also campaigning for their agenda, and they employed statistics and reports that stated that the potency and popularity of absinthe were responsible for the rise in the number of mental institution patients, suicides, and the general degradation of public health. In 1915, the temperance movement would claim victory over the Green Fairy as France banned both the production and sale of the beverage.

TRITTER RICKEY

SWISS WHITE ABSINTHE

1 OUNCE
FRESH LIME JUICE

¾ OUNCE
SUGAR SYRUP
[*page 24*]

4
FRESH MINT LEAVES

2 OUNCES
GIN

SODA WATER

SPRIGS OF FRESH MINT,
for garnish

*I*nvented by Michael Tritter, this cocktail is prepared by Aaron Polsky of White Star in New York City. Aaron unexpectedly fell in love with the restaurant business when he got a side job as a food runner at Thomas Keller's Bouchon Bakery in New York. From bakery to barroom, Aaron enjoys the journey this drink has taken and how it pairs the notable taste of Swiss white absinthe with gin and mint leaves.

Pour the absinthe into a chilled Collins glass. Swirl to coat the glass, then discard the remaining absinthe. Set the glass aside.

Pour the lime juice and sugar syrup into a cocktail shaker, and add the mint leaves. Muddle the mint for a few seconds, then add the gin. Fill the shaker with ice, and shake well. Fill the glass with ice and strain the drink into it. Top with soda. Garnish with a few sprigs of mint and a straw, and serve.

LAWHILL

2 OUNCES
RYE

❧

¾ OUNCE
DRY VERMOUTH

❧

¼ OUNCE
ABSINTHE VERTE

❧

1 DASH
MARASCHINO LIQUEUR

❧

1 DASH
ANGOSTURA BITTERS

This flavorful cocktail, which includes the distinct taste of rye with dashes of maraschino liqueur and Angostura bitters, is a favorite of its creator, John Gersten of Drink in Boston.

ABSINTHE WAS EMBROILED in the plot of the suspenseful 1998 movie *Deceiver*, as Tim Roth's character, James Walter Wayland, suggests that his recent consumption of absinthe is to blame for his memory problems.

Pour the rye, vermouth, absinthe, liqueur, and bitters into an iced cocktail shaker, and stir to combine. Strain the drink into a cocktail glass, and serve.

REMEMBER THE MAINE

2 OUNCES
RYE

¾ OUNCE
SWEET VERMOUTH

⅛ OUNCE
CHERRY HEERING

⅛ OUNCE **ABSINTHE**

1
BRANDIED CHERRY,
for garnish [*optional*]

*T*his rye-inspired cocktail was also developed by John Gersten of Drink in Boston. The sweet vermouth and Cheery Heering here work together to complement the absinthe.

Pour the rye, vermouth, Cheery Heering, and absinthe into an iced cocktail shaker, and stir to combine. Strain the drink into a cocktail glass. Garnish with the brandied cherry on the side of the glass, if desired, and serve.

THE THIRD DEGREE

2 OUNCES
PLYMOUTH GIN

—✦—

1 OUNCE
DRY VERMOUTH

—✦—

3 DASHES
ABSINTHE

*A*fter nine years of working in various positions at numerous restaurants, Ryan Fitzgerald eventually found himself with the opportunity to work behind the bar. For the past ten years, that's where he has remained, now bartending at Baretta in San Francisco. His passion for bartending led to the creation of this drink, which calls for Plymouth gin——the style of liquor, not the brand name.

Pour the gin, vermouth, and absinthe into a cocktail shaker filled with ice. Strain the drink into a chilled cocktail glass, and serve.

BABU

ABSINTHE

**1½ OUNCES
GABRIEL BOUDIER
SAFFRON-INFUSED GIN**

**½ OUNCE
ZUBROWKA BISON
GRASS VODKA**

**½ OUNCE
LEMON JUICE**

**¼ OUNCE
SIMPLE SYRUP**
[page 24]

**1
EGG WHITE**

SODA WATER

LONG LEMON PEEL,
for garnish

*T*imothy Bowman of Redd in the heart of Napa Valley, California, developed a seasonal drink repertoire to complement the restaurant's contemporary approach to Wine Country cuisine that offers serious food in an unpretentious, elegant atmosphere. This cocktail, with its earthy tones from Gabriel Boudier saffron-infused gin and Zubrowka bison grass vodka, is perfect for the spring and fall, when nature is in transition and organic fragrances fill the air.

Pour the absinthe into a tall cocktail glass. Swirl to coat the glass, and discard the remaining absinthe. Set glass aside.

Pour the gin, vodka, lemon juice, simple syrup, and egg white into a cocktail shaker. Hard shake for 30 seconds. Pour directly into the prepared glass and top with soda. Garnish the glass with a long strip of lemon peel, and serve.

"B" MONSTER

1½ OUNCES
LEOPOLD'S GIN

1½ OUNCES
FRESH GRAPEFRUIT JUICE

1 TABLESPOON
ST. GEORGE ABSINTHE

1 TABLESPOON
GRENADINE

1 STRIP OF
LIME PEEL,
for garnish

*M*arc Hartenfels of Bardessono in Napa Valley, California, offers this recipe that features handcrafted Leopold's gin and St. George absinthe. Marc recommends pairing this particular brand of gin and absinthe because both offer high-quality products that are diligently produced by artisans and not by corporate distilleries that mass-produce their spirits.

THE QUALITY of absinthe is still valued against pre-ban Pernod Fils absinthe, and bottles of the pre-ban product are so highly prized today that they sell for several thousands of dollars.

Pour the gin, grapefruit juice, absinthe, and grenadine into a cocktail shaker. Shake well, and strain the drink into a small cocktail glass. Garnish the glass with the strip of lime peel, and serve.

NORTH BY NORTHWEST

¾ OUNCE
FRESH LEMON JUICE

¾ OUNCE
SIMPLE SYRUP
[*page 24*]

¼ OUNCE
VIEUX PONTARLIER
ABSINTHE

1½ OUNCES
AVIATION GIN

CHAMPAGNE

This is Brian Miller's twist on the classic French 75. He was inspired by Cary Grant, who played Roger Thornhill in the classic Hitchcock film of the same name, and always wished he could've served him at the Oak Bar in the Plaza Hotel back in the day. If you'd like Brian to serve this drink to you, you can find him at Death + Company in New York City.

Pour the lemon juice, simple syrup, absinthe, and gin into a cocktail shaker. Shake well and strain the drink into a champagne flute. Top off with a splash of Champagne. Serve.

CEDAR SHINGLE

3 OUNCES
GIN

1½ OUNCES
ABSINTHE

SPLASH OF
VERMOUTH

SPLASH OF
GRAND MARNIER

CANDIED ORANGE PEELS,
for garnish

*N*antucket is known for its houses adorned in cedar shingle siding. This fall season drink from Sean S. Graves of Brant Point Grill at the famed White Elephant Resort, on the island off the coast of Massachusetts, pays homage to that fresh yellow color on a newly shingled house. You can find candied orange peels in specialty grocery stores.

Pour the gin, absinthe, and vermouth into a cocktail shaker filled with ice. Shake for about 20 seconds. Strain the drink into a chilled martini glass, and add the Grand Marnier. Garnish with candied orange peels, and serve.

RATTLESNAKE

ABSINTHE

2 OUNCES
**AMERICAN
RYE WHISKEY**

¾ OUNCE
FRESH LEMON JUICE

¾ OUNCE
SIMPLE SYRUP
[*page* 24]

1
EGG WHITE

*A*aron Polsky of White Star in New York City is a big fan of The Savoy Cocktail Book by Harry Craddock, first published in 1930, because it accounts for the true roots of America's most venerable cocktails. This respect for tradition inspired Aaron to create the Rattlesnake, which incorporates basic ingredients centered around a classic rye whiskey flavor.

Pour the absinthe into a chilled sour glass. Swirl to coat the glass, then discard the remaining absinthe. Set the glass aside.

Pour the rye whiskey, lemon juice, simple syrup, and egg white into a cocktail shaker. Shake vigorously. Add ice to the shaker, and shake vigorously again. Strain the drink into the prepared glass, and serve.

RATTLESNAKE FIZZ

2 OUNCES
RYE (80 PROOF)

¼ OUNCE
ABSINTHE

1 OUNCE
LEMON JUICE

1 TEASPOON
SUGAR

1
EGG WHITE

GINGER ALE

ANGOSTURA BITTERS

One night while he was experimenting in his "laboratory," Tim Stookey of Presidio Social Club in San Francisco came up with this concoction. While he liked it, he was at a loss for what to call it. A few days later, he was at the bar telling his friend about it, when this person says he thinks he's heard of it. Stookey pulls out his iPhone, punches in the ingredients, and up pops a recipe for the Rattlesnake. So much for originality, but it solved the naming problem. Yet there is one difference: Stookey added ginger ale, so he has no qualms about introducing this as the Rattlesnake Fizz.

Pour the rye, absinthe, lemon juice, sugar, and egg white into a cocktail shaker filled with ice. Shake vigorously. Strain the drink into a highball glass that is filled three-quarters with ice. Top off with ginger ale, and add a drop of Angostura bitters. Serve.

ROBERT BURNS
ON THE ROCKS

ABSINTHE

2 OUNCES
SCOTCH WHISKEY

¾ OUNCES
SWEET VERMOUTH

3 DROPS
ORANGE BITTERS

1
**CANDIED
MARASCA CHERRY,**
for garnish

*A*nother recipe from Aaron Polsky at White Star in New York City and his library of books featuring old-school recipes that have stood the test of time and changing tastes. Robert Burns on the Rocks, inspired by the pages of A. S. Crockett's The Old Waldorf-Astoria Bar Book, *features a classic blending of whiskey and sweet vermouth——two tastes found in the popular Rob Roy cocktail——and absinthe.*

Pour the absinthe into a chilled cocktail glass. Swirl to coat the glass, then discard the remaining absinthe. Set glass aside. Pour the scotch whiskey, vermouth, and orange bitters into a chilled cocktail shaker filled with freshly cracked ice, and stir to combine. Strain the drink into the prepared glass. Add a large chunk of ice. Garnish with the candied marasca cherry, and serve.

· LIQUEURS & ·
BITTERS

⎯ RECIPES ⎯

Absinthe was created to be a medicine. It evolved into an aperitif by being mixed with water, but was combined with other mixers——sugar, orgeat syrup, anisette, gum syrup——since early in the nineteenth century. While continuing to be consumed as an aperitif, it further evolved into an ingredient used in cocktails around the end of the nineteenth century. Its complex aromas lend well to cocktails, especially and particularly when in the hands of skilled mixologists. The popularity of the historic Sazerac, for example, serves as an illustration of how absinthe's herbal qualities combine beautifully with other alcohols for a refreshing drink.

Mixologists know that a successful cocktail is not just about taste——equally important are appearance and scent. Absinthe provides cocktails with an enticing look and aromatic presence before the beverage touches one's lips.

LOCAL SAZERAC

3 BIG DASHES
ST. GEORGE ABSINTHE

2 OUNCES
OSOCALIS BRANDY

¼ OUNCE
SIMPLE SYRUP
[*page 24*]

2 DASHES
PEYCHAUD'S BITTERS

LEMON ZEST

*T*he Sazerac is one of the oldest known cocktails, with its origins in pre-Civil War New Orleans. The original drink, created by Antoine Amédée Peychaud in the 1830s, is based on a combination of cognac and bitters and is reported to be the first cocktail ever invented in America. The cocktail was named by John Schiller in 1859 upon the opening of his Sazerac Coffee House in New Orleans. Both most likely derive their name from a popular brand of cognac, Sazerac de Forge et Fils. The recipe here is from Marc Hartenfels of Bardessono in Napa Valley, California.

Fill a bucket glass with ice and the dashes of absinthe. Set aside.

Pour the brandy, simple syrup, and bitters into a cocktail shaker, and stir to combine. Empty the ice from the prepared glass, and strain the drink into it. Twist the lemon zest over the glass and rub the rim. Discard the zest. Serve.

THE BITTERSWEET

1½ ounces
ABSINTHE

—❦—

½ ounce
CAMPARI

—❦—

½ ounce
GALLIANO

—❦—

½ ounce
BENEDICTINE

—❦—

2 dashes
ORANGE BITTERS

—❦—

½ ounce
WATER

—❦—

ORANGE PEEL,
for garnish

This recipe from Jason Littrell of the Randolph at Broome in New York City offers a unique blending on flavors and influences, from the herbal aromatics of absinthe, Benedictine, and sweet Galliano to the bitter essence of Campari.

IN 1992, Frances Ford Coppola directed *Dracula*, a film based on the 1897 novel by Bram Stoker featuring the vampire Count Dracula played by Gary Oldman. After Dracula rapes and drinks the blood of his reincarnated wife Mina's best friend, he seduces Mina over a glass of absinthe and says to her, "Absinthe is the aphrodisiac of the self. The green fairy who lives in the absinthe wants your soul. But you are safe with me."

Pour the absinthe, Campari, Galliano, Benedictine, bitters, and water into a cocktail shaker, and stir to combine. Strain into a rocks glass with one large piece of hand-cracked ice. Garnish with an orange peel, and serve.

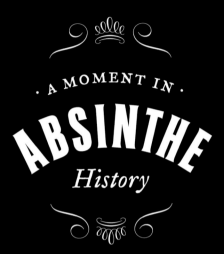

A MOMENT IN ABSINTHE History

The near-global ban of absinthe buried it in a grave of stigma and condemnation. The beverage faded away from social scenes around the world and was no longer drunk along the boulevards of Paris or the canals of New Orleans. Absinthe faded into obscurity. However, a small number of enthusiasts in the Val-de-Travers kept the legacy alive by preserving recipes, distilling practices, and vintage bottles. These clandestine artisans made the resurrection of absinthe possible.

After France and Switzerland banned the drink, many other nations adopted an "out of sight, out of mind" tolerance for it. Though genuine absinthe remained nearly impossible to find in most countries, true absinthe was never technically prohibited in places such as Australia, Spain, and Portugal. In fact, many of these countries continued to produce absinthe for local consumption. Absinthe kept a low profile for more than eight years, but in the 1990s, technology changed everything. The Internet brought together absinthe enthusiasts from across the planet and allowed for the exchange of unbiased information about absinthe. Stories of the green drink started to appear in online chat rooms in the early 1990s. The Green Fairy had found a new social platform where it could dispel the stigmas of the past. This renewed interest in the drink, however, resulted in the proliferation of fake absinthes, most notably from the Czech Republic in 1994. Unsuspecting buyers were sold product that gave them a false introduction to the taste and quality of real absinthe——an unfortunate result of the beverage's resurrection that still persists in today's marketplace. Nevertheless, by the mid-1990s the world's perception of absinthe had changed.

YESTERDAY'S SONG

1½ OUNCES
CABANA CACHAÇA

—❦—

½ OUNCE
FRESH LIME JUICE

—❦—

½ OUNCE
OBSELLO ABSINTHE

—❦—

¼ OUNCE
RUNNY HONEY

—❦—

¼ OUNCE
MARASCHINO LIQUOR

—❦—

1 DASH
ANGOSTURA BITTERS

—❦—

GINGER BEER

—❦—

FRESH ROSEMARY SPRIG,
for garnish

Though this shopping list is longer than most, don't be put off by it. Once you have the ingredients, you're just a few shakes away from being rewarded with a deliciously complex drink of rosemary, lime, and ginger beer, courtesy of Jeff Hollinger of Absinthe Brasserie & Bar in San Francisco.

Pour the cachaça, lime juice, absinthe, Runny Honey, liquor, and bitters into a cocktail shaker filled with ice. Shake for 20 to 30 seconds, or until well chilled. Strain the drink into a Collins glass filled with ice. Top with the ginger beer, and garnish with the rosemary sprig. Serve.

ARGENTO'S DREAM

1
EGG WHITE

¾ OUNCE
FRESH LEMON JUICE

¾ OUNCE
SIMPLE SYRUP
[page 24]

1 OUNCE
AMARO

¾ OUNCE
ABSINTHE VERTE

3 DASHES
PEYCHAUD'S BITTERS

Owner Hari Nathan Kalyan of the Randolph at Broome in New York City developed this absinthe recipe using egg white, lemon juice, and simple syrup—— a very creative combination.

TIM BURTON'S 1999 production of *Sleepy Hollow* features a constable named Ichabod Crane, played by Johnny Depp, who must solve mysterious murders taking place in 18th-century Sleepy Hollow. The constable drinks absinthe——but who wouldn't, given those circumstances?

In a cocktail shaker, whip the egg white with the lemon juice and simple syrup. Add the amaro and absinthe, and shake well. Pour into a glass filled with hand-cracked ice. Top with the bitters, and serve.

APPETIZER L'ITALIENNE

2 OUNCES
SWEET VERMOUTH

1 OUNCE
FERNET BRANCA

⅛ OUNCE
ABSINTHE BLANCHE

⅛ OUNCE
SIMPLE SYRUP
[*page 24*]

This recipe from John Gertsen of Drink in Boston has a distinct Italian influence from the sweet vermouth and Fernet Branca, which contributes a bitter, aromatic flavor to the herbal absinthe. These three flavors blend to offer a sense of old Italy full of earthly textures and balanced flavors.

Pour the vermouth, Fernet Branca, absinthe, and simple syrup into a cocktail shaker, and stir to combine. Strain the drink into a single rocks glass, and serve.

BLUE STEEL

2 OUNCES
AGED JAMAICAN RUM

½ OUNCE
CRÈME DE CASSIS

1 BARSPOON
RYE WHISKEY

2 DASHES
ANGOSTURA BITTERS

3 DASHES
ABSINTHE

THICK SLICE OF
LEMON PEEL,
for garnish

FRESH CILANTRO SPRIG,
for garnish

Serving short drinks in a tall glass, sans straw, is a favorite trick of Daniel Hyatt, a Michelin-recommended bartender for both 2009 and 2010, from San Francisco's Alembic. It encourages slow sipping and intensifies the aromatic experience. Blue Steel is one such drink, this one developed out of his love of the combination of berry flavors and absinthe. The sprig of cilantro is an ingenius, and delicious, finish.

Pour the rum, crème de cassis, rye whiskey, bitters, and absinthe into a highball glass. Add 3 or 4 large ice cubes and stir gently. Garnish with a thick slice of lemon peel and a small sprig of fresh cilantro. Serve.

HEART GROWS FONDER

1 OUNCE
KÜBLER ABSINTHE

¾ OUNCE
BLACKBERRY SYRUP

½ OUNCE
CRÈME DE VIOLETTE

In the heart of California's wine country, Erika Fey of Cyrus artfully balances the traditional preparation of absinthe with modern flavors, such as blackberry and violets.

THE FILM *From Hell* [2001] was based on the novel of the same name by Alan Moore and Eddie Campbell. The story, set in London in 1888, is about Jack the Ripper. Frederick Abberline, played by Johnny Depp, has psychic visions of the future with the help of opium and absinthe, and he uses these insights to help him solve the cases.

Pour absinthe into a rocks glass. Float the blackberry syrup over the absinthe, then float the crème de violette over the syrup. Place a serrated absinthe spoon on top of the glass with a large ice cube on top. Slowly drip ice water from an absinthe dripper over the ice cube. Once the portions of ice water and absinthe mixture are equal, stir the drink. Serve.

THE HERMITAGE

2 OUNCES
DEL MAGUEY CHICHICAPA MEZCAL

¼ OUNCE
LUXARDO MARASCHINO

¾ OUNCE
DUBONNET ROUGE

3 DASHES
GRAPEFRUIT BITTERS

3 DASHES
ABSINTHE

BROAD PIECE OF
GRAPEFRUIT ZEST,
for garnish

Ryan Fitzgerald has helped open a variety of notable bars in San Francisco, including Bourbon & Branch, Tres Agaves, and Beretta. Influential in the San Francisco cocktail scene, Fitzgerald is known for his inventive combinations such as the Hermitage, an absinthe recipe that dares to blend a flavor of Mexico via the Del Maguey Chichicapa mezcal with red wine-based Dubonnet rouge and the complexity of Luxardo maraschino.

Pour the mezcal, maraschino, Dubonnet rouge, bitters, and absinthe into a cocktail shaker filled with ice. Shake well, and strain the drink into a chilled cocktail glass. Garnish with the grapefruit zest, and serve.

FLOWERS OF DISTINCTION

1 OUNCE
DEL MAGUEY MEZCAL

—⋯—

1 OUNCE
LILLET ROUGE

—⋯—

1 OUNCE
**ST. GERMAIN
ELDERFLOWER LIQUEUR**

—⋯—

1 OUNCE
FRESH LEMON JUICE

—⋯—

DASH
ABSINTHE

This aptly named original cocktail, offered by Jason "Buffalo" Lograsso of Bourbon & Branch in San Francisco, is refreshing and feminine with a pleasantly strong, smoky backbone. All of the ingredients have some kind of floral connection, from the towering flower of the desert lily [from which mezcal is produced], to the stunning bright color and nuanced aromas of the lillet, to the lovely elderflower.

Pour the mezcal, lillet, elderflower liqueur, and lemon juice into a cocktail shaker. Shake well, and strain the drink into a cocktail glass. Add the dash of absinthe on the top of the drink, and serve.

5

MODERN

CLASSICS &
CUTTING EDGE

~ RECIPES ~

With flare and flamboyance, daring and swagger, and grit and inanity, the recipes in this chapter are all about pushing the limit. So experiment with these recipes——and perhaps mix a few of your own. Preparing and drinking absinthe is an art form, and all great art requires an element or recklessness. So break out your favorite absinthe, pop the Champagne, and try a few of the following recipes before concocting your own.

Consider absinthe a new and essential ingredient in your culinary cocktail arsenal. The best mixologists——both amateur and professional——are willing to test the boundaries of ingredients. With absinthe currently in its nascent stage on the American cocktail landscape, it is quite possible that the most popular absinthe drink has not been invented yet.

NIGHT PORTER

1 OUNCE
DOLIN BLANC VERMOUTH

— ❧ —

¾ OUNCE
PERNOD ABSINTHE

— ❧ —

¾ OUNCE
RUBY PORT

— ❧ —

½ OUNCE
BENESIN MEZCAL

— ❧ —

LEMON TWIST,
for garnish

*T*his cocktail recipe from Jeff Hollinger of Absinthe Brasserie & Bar in San Francisco offers the balanced richness of Dolin Blanc vermouth and its spicy, aromatic sensibility with Ruby port's claret color and Benesin mezcal's agave origins——a complex but rewarding blend of tastes and cultures.

Pour the vermouth, absinthe, port, and mezcal into a cocktail shaker filled with ice. Stir for 20 to 30 seconds, until well chilled. Strain the drink into a chilled cocktail glass. Garnish with the lemon twist, and serve.

GILL SANS

**DUPLAIS BLANCHE
ABSINTHE**

2 OUNCES
PLYMOUTH GIN

¾ OUNCE
MANZANILLA SHERRY

¼ OUNCE
MARASCHINO LIQUEUR

2 DASHES
ORANGE BITTERS

LEMON TWIST,
for garnish

Among its many charms, absinthe is also infinitely versatile, as Jeff Hollinger of San Francisco's Absinthe Brasserie & Bar had long discovered. In this drink, the flavors of absinthe are blended perfectly with Manzanilla sherry, which evokes southern Spain's briny seashore climate, the dry, almond DNA of maraschino liqueur, and the smoothness of Plymouth gin.

Pour the absinthe into a chilled cocktail glass. Swirl to coat the glass, then discard the remaining absinthe. Set the glass aside.

Pour the gin, sherry, liqueur, and bitters into a cocktail shaker filled with ice. Stir for 20 to 30 seconds, or until well chilled. Strain the drink into the prepared glass. Garnish with the lemon twist, and serve.

ABSINTHE FIZZ

1
EGG WHITE

1½ OUNCES
ABSINTHE BLANCHE

¾ OUNCE
LEMON JUICE

¾ OUNCE
SIMPLE SYRUP
[*page 24*]

SODA WATER

*F*rom the meticulous bartender John Gersten at *Drink in Boston, this absinthe recipe features classic fizz ingredients and highball-glass style.*

DIRECTOR BAZ LUHRMANN'S film *Moulin Rouge* [2001] relates the story of a glamorous yet seedy Moulin Rouge nightclub in 1899 Paris, featuring constant absinthe drinking, partying, sex, and drugs. Many of the characters are constantly high, and the "Green Fairy" [Kylie Minogue] makes her appearance as one of their drunken hallucinations.

Pour the egg white, absinthe, lemon juice, and simple syrup into a cocktail shaker, and shake well. Add ice, and shake vigorously. Strain the drink into a cocktail glass. Top the drink with soda water, and serve.

DEATH AT DUSK

½ OUNCE
CRÈME DE VIOLETTE

—❧—

5 OUNCES
SPARKLING WINE

—❧—

¼ OUNCE
ABSINTHE

—❧—

1
MARASCHINO CHERRY,
for garnish

*T*his is a version of the cocktail *Death in the Afternoon* [absinthe and champagne], which was created for a 1935 book of humorous cocktail riffs called *So Red the Nose, or Breath in the Afternoon. While Death in the Afternoon is a great name, San Francisco-based Neyah White, from Nopa, admits it is a little lacking as far as drinks go. The addition of crème de violette has a rounding effect and gives the drink some subtlety.*

Pour the crème de violette and wine into a flute. Float the absinthe on top, and garnish with a maraschino cherry. Serve.

SACRED HEART

1½ ounces
LA PINTA POMEGRANATE
LIQUEUR

—❧—

¾ ounce
PERNOD ABSINTHE

—❧—

½ ounce
LIMONCELLO

—❧—

¼ ounce
LEMON JUICE

—❧—

LEMON TWIST,
for garnish

*L*a Pinta pomegranate liqueur gives this drink its distinctive color and taste. The bold flavors were developed by Jeff Hollinger at San Francisco's Absinthe Brasserie & Bar.

Pour the pomegranate liqueur, absinthe, limoncello, and lemon juice into a cocktail shaker filled with ice. Shake for 10 to 15 seconds, until well chilled. Strain the drink into a chilled cocktail glass. Garnish with the lemon twist, and serve.

EMERALD SOUND
COCKTAIL

*T*he cocktail was inspired by a mint julep; this is the south Indian version. A refreshing drink, it is perfect for the spring or summer. The taste is layered, the peppery taste adding a little bit of heat. It looks fruity, but once you taste it, you get sweet, you get spice, you get a little bit of mint, and then the absinthe at the end, which really brings out all of the flavors. Created by Danny Louie, this and other exotic cocktails can be found at Dosa in San Francisco, where Danny is often behind the bar.

ABSINTHE RINSE
[*St. George absinthe preferred*]

—◆—

8
MINT LEAVES

—◆—

1½ OUNCES
DOMAINE DE CANTON

—◆—

1 OUNCE
RYE WHISKEY
[*Rittenhouse 100 proof rye preferred*]

¾ OUNCE
MANGO GASTRIQUE
[*recipe follows*]

—◆—

MANGO SLICE
SPEARED
WITH 3 CLOVES IN IT,
for garnish

—◆—

MINT SPRIG,
for garnish

Pour absinthe into a chilled old-fashioned glass. Swirl to coat the glass, then discard any remaining absinthe. Set the glass aside.

Put the mint, Domaine de Canton, rye, and Mango Gastrique into a cocktail shaker and fill three quarters full with ice. Shake well and strain the drink into the prepared glass that has been filled with crushed ice. Serve.

MANGO GASTRIQUE

MAKES ABOUT **1¾** CUPS

4 BIRD'S-EYE CHILES

2 CUPS **MANGO NECTAR**
such as Looza Mango Nectar

½ CUP **SUGAR**

½ CUP **CHAMPAGNE VINEGAR**

PINCH OF **KOSHER SALT**

Grind the chiles in a spice grinder.

Pour the mango nectar into a saucepan and add the chiles. Place the pan over medium heat and bring the mixture to a simmer. Add the sugar, vinegar, and salt, and stir until the sugar is dissolved. Simmer for 5 minutes. Remove the pan from the heat, and allow the mixture to cool. Strain the gastrique into an airtight container. Store, covered, in the refrigerator up to 7 days.

GREEN GODDESS

5
FRESH BASIL LEAVES

1½ OUNCES
SQUARE ONE CUCUMBER
ORGANIC VODKA

½ OUNCE
SIMPLE SYRUP
[page 24]

½ OUNCE
FRESH LIME JUICE

¼ OUNCE
ABSINTHE

1 SPRIG OF
FRESH THYME

*T*his wonderful drink is perfect for the summertime. Neyah White of Nopa in San Francisco, who created it, always uses Genevese basil because other varieties of basil can augment the licorice flavors.

Muddle the basil in a cocktail shaker until all the leaves are bruised. Add the vodka, simple syrup, lime juice, absinthe, and thyme sprig. Fill the shaker with ice and shake hard. Strain the drink into a chilled cocktail glass. Shake the thyme sprig dry, then use it as a garnish. Serve.

PASSION AND 'PAGNE

**1½ OUNCES
NAVAN**

**½ OUNCE
KÜBLER ABSINTHE**

**1½ OUNCES
PASSIONFRUIT PURÉE**

**1 OUNCE
BRUT CHAMPAGNE**

LIME TWIST

This simple yet pretty drink has a complex taste. After the tartness of the passionfruit and the sweetness of the cognac come the herbaceous qualities of absinthe. Sierra Zimei of Season Bar at the renowned Four Seasons Hotel, San Francisco, added the bubbles to make the drink even better.

SAN FRANCISCO hosts a rich culinary tradition and passionate cocktail culture. A trip to the city would not be complete without a visit to the speakeasy Bourbon & Branch [pictured opposite].

Pour the Navan, absinthe, and passionfruit purée into a cocktail shaker filled with ice. Shake well, and strain the drink into a Champagne flute. Top with the Champagne. Garnish with the lime twist, and serve.

MEMORY LAPSE

*F*rom *Jeff Hollinger of Absinthe Brasserie & Bar in San Francisco, this recipe is unique in that it calls for house-made grenadine and a whole egg. Hollinger prefers to make his own grenadine because he can tailor it to his personal taste. Plus, it's very simple. During autumn when the temperature cools, he likes to add warm spices like cinnamon and cloves to his recipe for a rich grenadine——something that is much more rich than the sweetened cherry juice most people are used to drinking.*

2 TO 3 LEAVES OF
FRESH BASIL,
torn into small pieces

❦

½ OUNCE
HOMEMADE GRENADINE
[recipe follows]

2 OUNCES
KÜBLER ABSINTHE

1
WHOLE EGG

❦

SODA WATER

Muddle the basil with the grenadine in a cocktail shaker. Add the absinthe and the egg, fill the shaker with ice, and shake vigorously for at least 30 seconds or until the mixture feels light. Strain the cocktail into a chilled absinthe glass, and top with soda water. Serve.

HOMEMADE
GRENADINE

MAKES ABOUT **1½** CUPS

2 CUPS **POMEGRANATE JUICE**

3 TO **4** STAR ANISE PODS

3 ALLSPICE BERRIES

3 WHOLE CLOVES

2 CINNAMON STICKS

½ TABLESPOON **SZECHUAN PEPPERCORNS,** *or to taste*

1 TO **2 DRIED RED CHILES,** *optional*

1 CUP **SUGAR**

In a small pot, combine the pomegranate juice with the spices and bring to a low boil. Cover the pot, remove it from the heat, and allow the spices to infuse into the juice for at least 15 minutes. Strain the juice through a fine sieve into a measuring cup. Return the juice and an equal measurement of sugar to the pot and heat until the sugar dissolves. Allow the finished grenadine to cool and transfer it into a container from which it can be poured. This drink tastes a bit like root beer. Like any syrup, it will keep two to three weeks in the refrigerator.

GREEN MONSTER

1 OUNCE
CRÈME DE MENTHE

1 OUNCE
ABSINTHE

1 OUNCE
HEAVY CREAM

FRESH MINT LEAVES,
for garnish

In homage to Boston's Fenway Park, this drink from Sean S. Graves of Nantucket's Brant Point Grill, at the famous White Elephant Resort, is a great summer drink, especially if you're watching the Red Sox on TV or the kids playing catch in the yard.

IN DIRECTOR STEPHEN SOMMERS'S film *Van Helsing* [2004], the main character Gabriel Van Helsing, played by Hugh Jackman, discovers the Frankenstein monster under a windmill crammed full with absinthe bottles. Van Helsing takes a few swigs of absinthe to calm his nerves——he is, after all, charged with the task of defeating evil, as well as serving as the archenemy to the mystical creature known as Dracula.

Pour the crème de menthe, absinthe, and heavy cream into a cocktail shaker filled with ice. Shake for about 20 seconds. Strain the drink into a rocks glass filled with ice. Garnish with mint leaves, and serve.

PROMISSORY NOTE

¾ OUNCE
DRY VERMOUTH

—❧—

¾ OUNCE
REPOSADO TEQUILA

—❧—

1 OUNCE
**DOMAINE DE CANTON
GINGER LIQUEUR**

—❧—

1 BARSPOON
HONEY

—❧—

2 TO 3 DASHES
ABSINTHE

—❧—

**FRESHLY GRATED
CINNAMON,**
for garnish

—❧—

THIN SLICE OF
RADISH,
for garnish

*D*aniel Hyatt of the Alembic in San Francisco says this cocktail was inspired by the dry spiciness of dry vermouth and Canton liqueur, which was the first thing he mixed when he tried absinthe. The cocktail retains the character of all the ingredients, but has a great balance and harmony as a whole.

Pour the vermouth, tequila, liqueur, honey, and absinthe in a cocktail shaker filled with cracked ice. Strain the drink into a chilled cocktail glass. Garnish with the cinnamon and radish slice, and serve.

THYME AND PUNISHMENT

ABSINTHE

5 SPRIGS OF
FRESH THYME

½ OUNCE
FRESH LEMON JUICE

½ OUNCE
FRESH LIME JUICE

¼ OUNCE
SIMPLE SYRUP
[*page 24*]

2 OUNCES
**TANQUERAY
RANGPUR GIN**

BITTER LEMON SODA

2 SPRIGS OF
FRESH THYME,
for garnish

*E*ven though there is a lot of citrus in this cocktail, the prevailing flavor is of the thyme. The absinthe adds a layer of complexity, much as you would use a bitter in a different style of drink. This fresh, simple cocktail comes to us from Timothy Bowman of Redd in Napa Valley.

Pour the absinthe into a tall cocktail glass. Swirl the glass to coat, then discard the remaining absinthe. Set the glass aside.

Muddle the thyme, lemon juice, lime juice, and simple syrup in a cocktail shaker. Add the gin. Shake well, and strain into the prepared glass. Top with the soda. Garnish with the additional thyme, and serve.

ABSINTHE
BUYING GUIDE

With more than two dozen absinthes approved for sale, whether domestic or imported, consumers have choices. As those numbers grow, the styles and quality will vary greatly.

This guide includes a website address for each entry so you can learn more about a particular brand and research other aspects of absinthe that may interest you. The websites provide a wealth of information, from prices to locations in your area where absinthe can be purchased.

$ = $30 to $50

$$ = $51 to $70

$$$ = $71 to $100

$$$$ = MORE THAN $100

DUPLAIS BLANCHE

WWW.TEMPUSFUGITSPIRITS.COM

Product of Switzerland

· IMPORTED BY ·
Tempus Fugit Spirits, Petaluma, California

· STYLE ·
Blanche [clear]

· ALCOHOL ·
60% [120 proof]

· DISTILLERY ·
Matter-Luginbühl, Kallnach, Switzerland

· COST ·
$$

Duplais Blanche is crystal clear with pewter reflections. Warm yet complexly herbal nose with hints of mentholated wormwood, ground coriander, and candied angelica root. When louched, it produces a cloud-white opalescent in the glass, tinged with pewter. Full mouth-feel, silky, yet subdued, it tastes of a complex, heady blend of medicinal herbs with a lingering anise-bright sweetness that coats and caresses the tongue. This authentic Suisse Absinthe Blanche is a great value and represents one of the best modern absinthes based on traditional recipes.

DUPLAIS VERTE

WWW.TEMPUSFUGITSPIRITS.COM

Product of Switzerland

· IMPORTED BY ·
Tempus Fugit Spirits, Petaluma, California

· STYLE ·
Verte [green colored]

· ALCOHOL ·
68% [136 proof]

· DISTILLERY ·
Matter-Luginbühl, Kallnach, Switzerland

· COST ·
$$$

In the glass, Duplais Verte has a very intense, pure tourmaline green color. When ice-cold water is slowly added, it releases a classic green-tinted, lightly billowing and opalescent louche. The aroma has subtle yet well-integrated wormwood notes with mint and alpine floral undertones. The taste is lightly creamy and crisp with a soothing anise and wormwood finish. At the current price, this authentic Suisse Absinthe Verte is a great value as it represents one of the best modern absinthes based on traditional recipes.

GERMAIN-ROBIN
ABSINTHE SUPÉRIEURE

WWW.GREENWAYDISTILLERS.COM

Product of the United States

· STYLE ·

Blanche [clear]

· ALCOHOL ·

45% [90 proof]

· DISTILLERY ·

Greenway Distillers, Ukiah, California

· COST ·

$$$

In the glass, Germain-Robin is colorless. Adding ice-cold water produces a milky-white louche. The aroma is star anise up front with fresh herbal undertones. The flavor is star anise with floral and spicy notes. It leaves a sweet-wormwood drynesss on the palate. At the current price, this all-natural authentic absinthe is a great value.

HERITAGE VERTE

WWW.TEMPUSFUGITSPIRITS.COM

Product of France

· IMPORTED BY ·

Tempus Fugit Spirits, Petaluma, California

· STYLE ·

Verte [green colored]

· ALCOHOL ·

68% [136 proof]

· DISTILLERY ·

Distillerie Paul Devoille, Fougerolles, France

· COST ·

$$

In the glass, Heritage Verte is a deep, well-infused amber green color. Adding ice-cold water produces an intensely thick, yet reflective louche that completely captures the undiluted color of clouds. After ice water is added, it gives off a deep perfume of wormwood, anise, and fennel, which balance its relaxing yet bittersweet headiness. At the current price, this authentic French absinthe is a great value.

KÜBLER SUPÉRIEURE

WWW.KUBLERABSINTHE.COM

Product of Switzerland

· IMPORTED BY ·

Altamar Brands, LLC,
Corona Del Mar, California

· STYLE ·

Blanche [clear]

· ALCOHOL ·

53% [106 proof]

· DISTILLERY ·

Distillerie Kübler, Môtiers, Switzerland

· COST ·

$$

In the glass, Kübler is colorless. Adding ice-cold water produces a milky white louche. The aroma is mainly anise up front with an undertone of wormwood and fennel. The taste is a well-balanced blend of wormwood, anise, and fennel. It leaves a slight sweetness on the palate, reminding, or should I say encouraging, you to take another sip. At the current price, this authentic Suisse Absinthe Blanche is an exceptional value.

LA CLANDESTINE SUPÉRIEURE

WWW.VIRIDIANSPIRITS.COM

Product of Switzerland

· IMPORTED BY ·

Viridian Spirits, Manhasset, New York

· STYLE ·

Blanche [clear]

· ALCOHOL ·

53% [106 proof]

· DISTILLERY ·

Claude-Alain Bugnon, Couvet, Switzerland

· COST ·

$$$

In the glass, La Clandestine is colorless. Adding ice-cold water produces an opaque milky-white louche. The aroma is a bold blend of wormwood, anise, and fennel with herbal undertones. The taste is anise up front, with wormwood at the surface. The choice of herbs gives this absinthe a natural sweetness; adding a sugar cube at the drip may be too much. At the current price, this well-made authentic Suisse Absinthe Blanche is an exceptional value.

LA FÉE ABSINTHE PARISIENNE

WWW.LAFEE.COM

Product of France

· IMPORTED BY ·

Green Utopia, Manhasset, New York

· STYLE ·

Verte [green colored]

· ALCOHOL ·

68% [136 proof]

· DISTILLERY ·

La Fée, Paris, France

· COST ·

$$

In the glass, La Fée Parisienne is a lime-green color. Adding ice cold water produces a milky lime-green louche. The aroma after louche is mostly anise with wormwood below the surface. The flavor of anise stands out, with noticeable numbing on the tongue from the star anise. At the current price, this absinthe is an average value.

LEOPOLD BROS. VERTE

WWW.LEOPOLDBROS.COM

Product of the United States

· STYLE ·

Verte [green colored]

· ALCOHOL ·

65% [130 proof]

· DISTILLERY ·

Leopold Bros., Denver, Colorado

· COST ·

$$$

In the glass, Leopold Bros. Verte is a dark olive color. Adding ice-cold water produces a thick pale yellowish green louche. The aroma is fresh wormwood with citrusy hints. The flavor is predominantly wormwood on top with anise and fennel just under the surface. It is a bit sweet if dripped with a sugar cube. At the current price, this authentic absinthe is a good value. This absinthe is for experienced absintheurs with sophisticated palates. We think this product has potential.

LUCID SUPÉRIEURE

WWW.DRINKLUCID.COM

Product of France

· IMPORTED BY ·

Viridian Spirits, Manhasset, New York

· STYLE ·

Verte [green colored]

· ALCOHOL ·

62% [124 proof]

· DISTILLERY ·

Distillerie Combier, Saumur, France

· COST ·

$$

In the glass, Lucid is a pale yellow and slightly clouded. Adding ice-cold water produces a nice opalescent milky white louche. The aroma is fresh with the anise-to-fennel ratio being well proportioned. The taste has an underlying herbal complexity that doesn't oversaturate the senses. It has a hint of wormwood bitterness that satisfies the palate. It's a good choice for first-time buyers looking to gain an appreciation of classic French absinthe. At the current price, this authentic absinthe is an exceptional value.

MANSINTHE BY MARILYN MANSON

WWW.TEMPUSFUGITSPIRITS.COM

Product of Switzerland

· IMPORTED BY ·

Tempus Fugit Spirits, Petaluma, California

· STYLE ·

Verte [green colored]

· ALCOHOL ·

66.6% [133.2 proof]

· DISTILLERY ·

Matter-Luginbühl, Kallnach, Switzerland

· COST ·

$$

In the glass, Mansinthe has an unusual, unique, yet natural green tint with light blue reflections. A slow-forming louche gives way to a thick green then white opalescence. Earthy, warm aromas, deep and musky, combine with light notes of alpine herbs and flowers. Initial flavors are round and savory with a full, buttery palate giving way to a balanced, refreshing, and complex finish. At the current price, this authentic Suisse absinthe is a great value.

MATA HARI BOHEMIAN

WWW.ABSINTHE.AT

Product of Austria

· IMPORTED BY ·
Fischer Schnapps, Manhasset, New York

· STYLE ·
Verte [green colored]

· ALCOHOL ·
60% [120 proof]

· DISTILLERY ·
Fischer Schnapps, Vienna, Austria

· COST ·
$$

In the bottle, Mata Hari is emerald green. Adding ice-cold water gradually produces a nice louche. The aroma has a candylike characteristic with wormwood undertones. The spicy taste masks the other herbs. At the current price, this absinthe is an average value.

NOUVELLE-ORLÉANS SUPÉRIEURE

WWW.VIRIDIANSPIRITS.COM

Product of France

· IMPORTED BY ·
Viridian Spirits, Manhasset, New York

· STYLE ·
Verte [green colored]

· ALCOHOL ·
68% [136 proof]

· DISTILLERY ·
Distillerie Combier, Saumur, France

· COST ·
$$$$

In the glass, Nouvelle-Orléans has a rich natural green color. Adding ice-cold water gradually produces a thick white opaque louche. It has a soft floral aroma that is refreshing and well balanced. The taste is lightly creamy and sweet with a soothing anise-and-wormwood finish. At the current price, this authentic French Belle Époque-style absinthe is an exceptional value.

OBSELLO VERTE

WWW.OBSELLO.COM
Product of Spain

· IMPORTED BY ·
Esmeralda Liquors, Manhasset, New York

· STYLE ·
Verte [green colored]

· ALCOHOL ·
50% [100 proof]

· DISTILLERY ·
Esmeralda Liquors Distillery, Lleida, Spain

· COST ·
$

In the glass, Obsello Verte is a natural-looking lime green. Adding ice-cold water quickly produces a nice cloudy louche. The aroma is fresh and minty with an anise top note with wormwood just below the surface. The taste is rich and creamy, and the mint adds a nice fresh finish. First-time buyers will enjoy the fresh herbs and rich flavors found in this classic Spanish absinthe. At the current price, this authentic Spanish absinthe is an exceptional value.

PACIFIQUE VERTE SUPÉRIEURE

WWW.TEMPUSFUGITSPIRITS.COM
Product of the United States

· DISTRIBUTED BY ·
Tempus Fugit Spirits, Petaluma, California

· STYLE ·
Verte [green colored]

· ALCOHOL ·
62% [124 proof]

· DISTILLERY ·
Pacific Distillery, Woodinville, Washington

· COST ·
$$

In the glass, Pacifique Verte has a light, crystalline peridot green color. Brisk and intense nose with a warm spiciness blended with crisp alpine notes, a classic, southern French/Swiss profile. The mouth-feel is brisk yet herbal with a complex and clean flavor tinged with ozone notes. The finish is long and pensive. At the current price, this authentic absinthe is an exceptional value.

PERNOD AUX PLANTES
D'ABSINTHE SUPÉRIEURE

WWW.PERNOD-RICARD-USA.COM

Product of France

· IMPORTED BY ·
Pernod Ricard USA, Purchase, New York

· STYLE ·
Verte [green colored]

· ALCOHOL ·
68% [136 proof]

· COST ·
$$

In the bottle, Pernod is a light olive-green color. Adding ice-cold water produces a pale-green louche. The aroma is subdued and mainly anise. The flavor is anise and lemon balm. Any hint of wormwood is not worth mentioning. First-time buyers can enjoy the experience of drinking Pernod, the namesake that launched the absinthe industry more than two hundred years ago. At the current price, this absinthe is a good value.

SIRÉNE VERTE

WWW.NORTHSHOREDISTILLERY.COM

Product of the United States

· STYLE ·
Verte [green colored]

· ALCOHOL ·
60% [120 proof]

· DISTILLERY ·
North Shore Distillery, Lake Bluff, Illinois

· COST ·
$$

In the bottle, Siréne Verte is olive green. Adding ice-cold water produces a pale-yellow louche. The aroma has a top note of anise and wormwood with fennel just below the surface. The taste is predominantly star anise, which masks the other herbs. This absinthe is sweet; adding a sugar cube at the drip may push it over the line. The anethole concentration leaves the tongue comfortably numb. At the current price, this authentic absinthe is a good value.

VIEUX·CARRE SUPÉRIEURE

WWW.VIEUXCARREABSINTHE.COM
Product of the United States

· STYLE ·
Verte [green colored]

· ALCOHOL ·
60% [120 proof]

· DISTILLERY ·
Philadelphia Distilling,
Philadelphia, Pennsylvania

· COST ·
$$

In the bottle, Vieux-Carre is a darker yellow-green color. Adding ice-cold water produces a pale yellow-green louche. The aroma is fresh wormwood with anise and fennel just below the surface. The taste starts out with wormwood bitterness followed by fennel-with-mint undertones. At the current price, this authentic absinthe is a great value.

VIEUX PONTARLIER ABSINTHE
FRANÇAISE SUPÉRIEURE

WWW.TEMPUSFUGITSPIRITS.COM
Product of France

· IMPORTED BY ·
Tempus Fugit Spirits, Petaluma, California

· STYLE ·
Verte [green colored]

· ALCOHOL ·
65% [130 proof]

· DISTILLERY ·
Distillerie Les Fils d'Emile Pernot,
Pontarlier, France

· COST ·
$$$

In the glass, Vieux Pontarlier is pale peridot green. Slowly dripping ice-cold water produces a lightly green-tinged and billowy opalescent louche. The aroma is fresh yet slightly briny and spicy with lightly mentholated notes. The flavors are multilayered, with subtle herbal undertones, and the anise and fennel are well balanced with a mentholated wormwood note. This authentic absinthe has been considered by a well-regarded critic as "the Gold Standard for the Absinthe category."

SHANE TISON

DANIEL HYATT

SCOTT BAIRD

NEYAH WHITE

MAE LANE

AARON POLSKY

MELISSA SHEPPARD

ERIC ALPERIN

JEFF HOLLINGER

CONTRIBUTORS

ERIK ADKINS Adkins is responsible for the bar programs at the Slanted Door and Heaven's Dog in San Francisco. He consulted on the bar for Oakland's Flora and his drinks have appeared in the *San Francisco Chronicle, New York Times, GQ, Food and Wine, San Francisco Magazine,* and *7x7.*

ERIC ALPERIN Having relocated three years ago from New York City to Los Angeles, Alperin feels fortunate to have found a small, passionate, and ever-growing cocktail community. He has worked with Sasha Petraske at Milk & Honey and Little Branch, both in NYC. Most recently they partnered to open The Varnish in downtown Los Angeles.

SCOTT BAIRD Cofounder of the Bon Vivants and owner of 15 Romolo, Baird, a lover of art in many forms, has worked jobs as diverse as florist, caterer, window display designer, and welder. As testament to his versatile, creative nature, he finds a way to implement his artistic eye in all of his work.

TIMOTHY BOWMAN Bowman showcases his fourteen years of experience with updated classics and a collection of cocktails inspired by the seasons at Redd, in the heart of the Napa Valley. In 2003, his East Coast training landed him a position at Auberge du Soleil, where he met critically acclaimed executive chef Richard Reddington.

JACKSON CANNON Together with three esteemed colleagues, Cannon formed the Jack Rose Society, dedicated to preserving the legacy of the art of the American cocktail. He has been featured in *Boston Magazine, Imbibe Magazine,* the *Boston Globe,* and the *Beverage Journal.* His cocktail program at Eastern Standard has received national attention from *USA Today* and Bacardi International.

RYAN FITZGERALD After working in all different areas of all kinds of different restaurants, Fitzgerald finally got the opportunity to get behind the bar, and for the past ten years that's where he and his passion have remained. That decade has seen him work at a variety of notable bars in San Francisco, including Bourbon & Branch, Tres Agaves, and Beretta.

ERIKA FEY Fey features expertly crafted classic cocktails on her menu at Cyrus, frequently drawing inspiration from the bounty of spectacular seasonal ingredients available from local Sonoma County farms to create unique cocktails with playful and surprising flavors and combinations.

LIZA GERSHMAN An award-winning photographer and writer, Gershman splits her time between San Francisco and the Napa Valley. She is a lover of travel with a fondness for the emerging cocktail movement, and her work has appeared in many publications, including the *San Francisco Chronicle, St. Helena Star, Calistoga Tribune, Datebook, Marin Magazine, 7x7, Drink Me,* and *Wine X.*

JOHN GERSTEN Regarded as one of Boston's most talented bartenders, Drink bar manager John Gertsen is also recognized locally and nationally as an expert on the history of cocktails. For several years, he served as an integral part of the No.9 Park bar program, before collaborating with Chef Barbara Lynch on the opening of Drink.

SEAN S. GRAVES Graves's passion for mixology started with inventing drinks for his college roommates while he studied hospitality management at the University of Kansas. In 2005, he moved to Nantucket and worked various management positions at Nantucket Island Resorts but could not resist the allure of the bar. Last spring, he was appointed beverage supervisor at Brant Point Grill in the White Elephant.

JOSH HARRIS Josh Harris, twenty-eight, is a San Francisco native inspired by the culinary arts and those eras that have come before this one. Harris, himself a bon vivant, is the founding partner of the consulting company the Bon Vivants. You can find him behind the bar at 15 Romolo in San Francisco.

MARC HARTENFELS Hartenfels believes that generous service is the heart of the hospitality industry. The German-born restaurant specialist has served in the kitchens, behind the bar, and on the restaurant floors of some of the world's most respected resorts and hotels, including the Mandarin Oriental in London's Hyde Park and Napa Valley's Auberge du Soleil. Hartenfels embodies the idea that simple materials that are elevated and made by hand turn out the very best drinks.

JONATHAN HENSON Henson's first food service job was as a dishwasher for a catering company on Martha's Vineyard in Massachusetts. His break came when he filled in for a sick bartender. A few cocktails and much research later, Henson found he had a talent for making drinks and entertaining guests, and loved it.

JEFF HOLLINGER Hollinger is manager of Absinthe Brasserie & Bar in San Francisco, where he oversees all aspects of the restaurant. He enhanced Absinthe's classically driven cocktail philosophy by introducing cocktail concepts using seasonal fresh ingredients and balancing flavors of both old and new ingredients, developing fresh cocktail recipes and resurrecting forgotten classics.

DANIEL HYATT Bay Area native Daniel Hyatt began his restaurant career as a teenager washing dishes and working in kitchens in Portland, Oregon. Most recently, in 2006, he opened the Alembic Bar in San Francisco with brewer and restaurateur David Mclean. His cocktails have been featured in numerous local and national publications.

HARI NATHAN KALYAN Kalyan is the owner of the Randolph on Broome, between Bowery and Elizabeth, in New York City.

MAE LANE Lane is a very colorful character. Apart from being a mixologist at Griffou, she is a country singer who loves the forties and dresses accordingly. She previously worked at Stanton Social as well as a few other popular New York venues.

JASON LITTRELL As the beverage director of the Randolph at Broome, Littrell relishes the opportunity to troll Chinatown searching for unusual ingredients. Under Sasha Petraske's tutelage, he developed his signature style, which is equal parts great drink and great delivery.

JASON "BUFFALO" LOGRASSO Buffalo became enchanted with San Francisco's food and drink culture on a visit in 2006. He first cut his teeth behind the bar at Coco500, going on to help open Oakland's Flora, Beretta in San Francisco, and the Alembic. He currently barkeeps at Bourbon & Branch.

DANNY LOUIE Native of San Francisco, Louie has been honing his craft in the art of cocktails in the top bars for three years. Experimenting in everything from the avante garde to the classic, he enjoys synthesizing unique ingredients. Louie tends bar at Dosa on Fillmore and the Alembic.

COLIN MCCARTHY Former bistro and bar manager at the Auberge du Soleil, McCarthy oversaw the design aspects of each cocktail menu at the resort's restaurant, Bistro and La Plage Pool bar, which reflected his extensive research in the traditions of classic concoctions and cutting-edge creations. He took his creativity east and opened Brinkley, a restaurant in New York City.

JIM MEEHAN Meehan's fifteen-year career behind the bar spans from Madison, Wisconsin, to New York City. He has compiled the latest recipes for *Mr. Boston's Bartending Guide*, *Food & Wine*'s annual cocktail book, and writes a column for *Sommelier Journal*. He is the general manager of PDT.

BRIAN MILLER Miller has been working behind the stick in bars and restaurants in New York City for fifteen years. He has been quietly honing his craft in the East Village at Death + Company, where he is now head bartender. Miller recently started his own consulting company, Double Windsor Inc.

AARON POLSKY Polsky began his career with a side job as a food runner opening Thomas Keller's Bouchon Bakery in New York. He later went on to study at culinary school in Paris, and returned to work at other New York restaurants before starting as a host at Sasha Petraske's Milk and Honey. In 2008, Petraske trained him to bartend at White Star.

PAUL SCANDURA At the age of fifteen, Scandura was hired by Joseph Fretta, who trained him in homemade charcuterie, fresh sausages, and cheeses. Scandura continued his education at the Culinary Institute of America, where he received his degree and was bitten by the wine bug. He is currently the spirits program director of Martini House.

PETER SCHAF Schaf has been described by cutting-edge food writer Louisa Chu as "the epicenter of the global absinthe revival" and is one of the most influential behind-the-scenes players in the modern absinthe renaissance. He is a self-taught absinthe historian and "distiller by experience." Schaf currently resides in Paris.

MELISSA SHEPPARD Originally from Manchester, New Hampshire, Sheppard moved to California in 2008. She's been bartending for more than eight years, despite having a degree in exercise science. Mixing drinks is her forte. And she enjoys what California has to offer in terms of outdoor activities and, of course, what she considers the incredible wine and food.

TIM STOOKEY After being a bellman there, Stookey was first asked to bartend at the Cafe Majestic in the Hotel Majestic in San Francisco. When the hotel was sold seven years later and Stookey found himself jobless at Christmastime, he was hired by Thad Vogler at the Presidio Social Club, where he has been ever since.

MARCOS TELLO At the Edison in downtown Los Angeles, Tello can be found trying to bring nostalgia to life. The Edison is home to burlesque shows, fire dancers, and fluttering Green Fairies.

SHANE TISON A proud native of rural Texas, Tison and his drinks have been featured in such publications as *Vanity Fair, Houston Modern Luxury,* and *Food and Beverage.* He is well recognized for cocktail creations for a number of prestigious fashion events in New York and around the world.

JOHN TROIA The owner and cofounder of Tempus Fugit Spirits, Troia is a leading expert on absinthe and has been directly involved in bringing the best, award-winning absinthes to the U.S. market. In addition to developing and producing some of the finest absinthe accessories on the market, he has amassed perhaps the finest vintage absinthe poster collection in the world. Troia spends much of his time traveling throughout the United States for trainings and seminars for numerous distributors, bars, and restaurants.

NEYAH WHITE White is currently the bar manager at Nopa in San Francisco, where his program is well respected for its array of house-produced bitters, tinctures, and liqueurs. He believes in a passive approach to menu setting where the local farms and orchards determine what is used by season rather than forcing ingredients into drinks.

SIERRA ZIMEI For the past thirteen years, Zimei has been passionate about two things: traveling and bartending——one puts her in debt, and the other pulls her out. When she's not traveling, she can be found behind the bar at the Four Seasons in San Francisco.

INDEX